FAITH AND REASON IN KIERKEGAARD

F. Russell Sullivan, Jr.

University Press of America

Copyright © 1978 by

University Press of America, Inc.™

4710 Auth Place, S.E., Washington, D.C. 20023

All rights reserved

Printed in the United States of America

ISBN: 0-8191-0559-7

B
4378
F35
S8

3 3001 00700 9698

Library of Congress Catalog Card Number: 78-60695

For

JUDITH ANN

RUSTY   DAVID

SCOTT   PAUL

ACKNOWLEDGEMENTS

My interest in Kierkegaard grew out of a long standing conviction that he was not a wild-eyed advocate of the absurdity of faith, and that criticisms of him as such from respected philosophical sources did not stand up under a careful and scholarly analysis of his works. I am indebted to Professor Bernard Elevitch of the philosophy department at Boston University who extended himself on my behalf at a very trying and crucial stage of his professional career. His efforts were invaluable in the difficult task that beset me: to show that such an unorthodox pleader of the Christian faith is, in reality, writing (albeit implicibly) to delineate how the movement of faith is a reasonable one. My deep appreciation also to Professors John Lavely, Nancy Lewis, Roger Richards and Sheila Shively for their support.

Finally, words are inadequate to express the feelings of indebtedness to my wife, Judith Ann. Since I began my career in Philosophy in 1966, she has been a constant source of support. During this period, three of our sons were born. The nature of that support has been given added meaning in that, despite the loss of two of our sons, her devotion and steadfastness did not diminish. It is primarily to her I dedicate this work.

INTRODUCTION

The purpose of this work is to clarify Kierkegaard's use of reason in the act of faith and to distinguish the special sense of "reason" that must be understood to appreciate fully Kierkegaard's purpose in writing. I hope to show that Kierkegaard does not denigrate every use of reason in the act of faith; in actuality he sees faith as a reasonable enterprise based on the human predicament. As we shall see, it is Kierkegaard's intent to persuade those whom he considers nominal Christians (because they appreciate only the doctrinal value of faith) to appreciate faith as a viable alternative to the spiritless condition that Kierkegaard feels permeates their lives. His aim is to present Christianity in a new light to those of his age. An authentic movement of faith is the result of individual self-awareness (sin). Only then can faith be assessed as the reasonable act of choosing Christ rather than the continuation of an inauthentic mode of existing (sin). The reasonableness of faith consists in nominal Christians envisaging it as a prudential choice, rather than as the result of understanding the historical and doctrinal aspects of Christianity. In truth, Kierkegaard sees the latter as secondary. Faith is, in this sense, not the result of a logical argument which supports the fact of the God-man in history. For Kierkegaard, no argument pro or contra can be convincing in this regard. Faith, then, is alogical on the doctrinal level. The fact of the Incarnation cannot be comprehended as true or false by means of logical argumentation. Although reason recognizes its own limitations, it is confronted with the evidence of sin and the Christian message, which essentially is a dialogue between Christ and man concerning this spiritual condition. Faith, then, is not just a reasonable wager in the Pascalian sense. Reason points to faith as a possible answer to man's predicament despite its limitations in reaching logical certainty concerning the doctrines of faith. Therefore, on the more important level, that of encountering and opting for Christianity once a true assessment of self is made, faith is a reasonable undertaking, though not a logical one in the above sense.

To support my view that Kierkegaard's view of Christian faith is reasonable, I must distinguish the disparate purposes of Kierkegaard's aesthetic (pseudonymous) writings and his non-aesthetic ones (Chapter I). In the former, Kierkegaard's intention to counter what he considers nominal Christianity has led him at times to posit faith as absurd, against the understanding. I shall argue that Kierkegaard does not consider faith as such. Assertions of this kind are Kierkegaard's attempt to persuade the Christian of his day that faith is not reached by means of logic or accumulated historical evidence; for him the fact of the God-man in history cannot be understood pro or contra. Faith is essentially an act of willing. How, then, does Kierkegaard's assessment of the alogical character of Christian faith lead him to grasp it as an essentially reasonable option? Kierkegaard's psychological works The Concept of Dread and The Sickness Unto Death are the first evidence of Kierkegaard's assessment of faith as reasonable (Chapter II).

Kierkegaard hopes that introspective evidence will lead individuals to an awareness of sin. For Kierkegaard, man is not only in sin; he is dominated by it; man can do nothing about his inauthentic state. Though Christians have an appreciation of the doctrinal value of Christianity, any viable faith must have as a necessary condition their individual awareness of sin; this is gained only by seeing that authentic Christianity begins with introspection and its resultant insights. Kierkegaard sees that only by having nominal Christians view Christianity as alogical in nature on the doctrinal level and themselves as inauthentic (dominated by sin) can they begin to will a change in their beings. Through his aesthetic and psychological works, Kierkegaard hopes to have shown that there is no logical or existential avenue to authenticity. Neither man's understanding of the tenets of faith nor his own unaided willed action can effect a change in his inauthentic state.

In my analysis of some of Kierkegaard's religious works (Chapter III), I shall present evidence of Kierkegaard's envisaging Christianity as just this reasonable alternative to man's existential and logical predicament. Although logic fails and he himself can do nothing concerning his state, the nominal Christian has the opportunity to will a change in his being by opting for the escape that Christianity offers. The Incarnation cannot be defended on logical grounds, but faith in Christ as a possible remedy for the sinful nature of man and as the only viable alternative for those Christians of his day is reasonable.

Kierkegaard's unique notion of subjectivity is now seen as an effective tool in his attempt to have the Christians of his day view faith as a reasonable undertaking (Chapter IV). For Kierkegaard, subjectivity is not truth; he feels, however, that introspection, i.e., subjectivity, can lead to beneficial results. He hopes that man might see himself as without existential supports for his spiritually helpless position. And, subjectivity must also be stressed in order to counter what Kierkegaard considers nominal Christianity. Even Kierkegaard's notion of ethical subjectivity in his aesthetic work Either-Or is easily misunderstood. I hope to show that Kierkegaard is not interested in presenting the value of the ethical life, but is only hopeful of having nominal Christians begin the introspective movement so that the reasonable aspect of faith can be gleaned by such individuals.

My conclusion (Chapter V) is an explication of Kierkegaard's assessment of faith as reasonable, which evolves from my analysis in the first four chapters. It is important to stress the fact that Kierkegaard is not interested in advancing the truth of Christianity vis-à-vis any other faith. He is writing only for those nominal Christians who have at least a modicum of appreciation of Christian doctrine. Kierkegaard sees Christian faith as a risk, but he is attempting to make his readers see that risk as a calculated one. Christian truth, of which Kierkegaard is convinced, must initially be won by an act that has only the motivation of a potential cure for the spiritual crisis at hand. But Kierkegaard thinks this is enough. His purpose in writing is to afford those existents who have come to terms with their spiritual condition an opportunity to see Christ as a possible Healer, and to will accordingly.

Kierkegaard's justification of faith in Christ is one that consists of two exclusive alternatives for the individuals whom he hopes to have drawn to an awareness of their spiritual plight. A confrontation with these two options--the possible discovery of authentic selfhood through the leap of faith as opposed to the continuation of one's inauthentic state of being--is the aim of Kierkegaard's explication of the notions of the paradoxical nature of faith, dread, despair and subjectivity.

Although I shall rely heavily upon primary sources in the development of my thesis, I have found contemporary philosophical critiques on the matter of the relationship between faith and reason in Kierkegaard plentiful, as well as relevant. As regards selecting material (secondary sources) for my particular thesis, the criteria I used in judging the merits of the critiques are: (1) was a derogatory judgment of Kierkegaard based on a one-sided view of him, i.e., did a philosopher concentrate only on the aesthetic works? In such a case (e.g., Blanshard, Chisholm), I consider the source useful in that part of my purpose is to defend Kierkegaard's meaning of reason against those who have judged him without a proper assessment of his religious works; (2) did a philosopher adequately see the problem of faith and reason in Kierkegaard as the result of not evaluating adequately the corpus of Kierkegaard's works (e.g., McKinnon, Søe)? and, (3) did a philosopher assess Kierkegaard's notion of the relationship between faith and reason somewhat in the same way I did (e.g., Allison, Garelick)? I will argue that Kierkegaard's notion of the reasonableness of faith is one based on the limits of reason (logic) to deal adequately with the doctrines of faith, as well as man's limitations to attain authenticity (an escape from the state of sin) by his own unaided, willed efforts. Kierkegaard's notion of reason is inextricably tied in with that of this recalcitrance of the will. Christianity is primarily a dialogue between Christ and desparing man. Christ directs his appeal to those who will recognize their spiritual condition and will to act upon it. Reason attests to its own limits in regard to doctrinal faith (logic and speculative thought), but it also can point to that which is a reasonable step even when reason (logic) itself is of no avail.

CHAPTER I

THE AESTHETIC WORKS

An initial problem in dealing with Kierkegaard's notions of faith and reason is the fact that his earlier works are pseudonymous and only in the last part of his life did he write under his own name.[1] Most of these pseudonymous works are commonly called "aesthetic"[2] because rather than writing directly concerning Christian faith, Kierkegaard writes in defense of the aesthetic and ethical levels of existence, as well as that level he calls "Religiousness A" in Concluding Unscientific Postscript. It is not my purpose to give a complete exposition of these levels (although a brief outline is needed) but to show that a positing of Kierkegaard's precise notion of reason in regard to the Christian act of faith must first encounter Kierkegaard's overt admittance of the irrational nature of faith that can be gleaned from some of these aesthetic works. Only then can we begin to assess in what sense Kierkegaard considered Christian faith reasonable and what specific argument he was actually presenting to support it as such to the Christians of his day. Section A of this chapter includes: (1) a brief exposition of the levels of existence; (2) a determination that Kierkegaard's notions of reason and faith within the context of these levels point to obvious inconsistencies; (3) a tentative conclusion gleaned from the above that Kierkegaard is not an irrationalist. Section B will be concerned with Kierkegaard's specific motive in presenting himself as against the understanding, and in what sense this is to be evaluated.

A. Faith as Illogical

The charge against Kierkegaard that he views faith as illogical rests upon what he himself has said in his aesthetic

---

[1] From 1843 to 1846 Kierkegaard's works are mainly pseudonymous. His various Edifying Discourses are the important exceptions. From 1847 on, Kierkegaard uses his own authorship except in Sickness Unto Death (1849) and Training in Christianity (1850).

[2] Besides the two aforementioned works, Kierkegaard's Concept of Dread (1844) is the other non-aesthetic pseudonymous work.

works. Before we meet these charges, it is important to note that Kierkegaard speaks as if Christian faith was the last stage in an existent's[1] ascent from the lowest level of existence, the aesthetic, through the ethical level and the level of Religiousness A to the level of Christian faith, Religiousness B. Thus, although in some of his aesthetic works he is purported to be advancing the "leap of faith" as if it were discontinuous with the lower levels of existence, he is at the same time, in other aesthetic works, leaving us open to interpret Christian faith as if it were continuous with them and, hence, not an irrational leap at all. Why the seeming contradiction? The answer will allow us to begin to grasp Kierkegaard's real intention in writing pseudonymously and help answer the charge of irrationalism. Let us, then, briefly depict Kierkegaard's levels of existence.

For Kierkegaard, the aesthetic life is the life of immediacy. It is essentially a life of not choosing: "The aesthetic choice is either entirely immediate and to that extent no choice, or it loses itself in the multifarious."[2] The aesthetic choice is no real choice because it is always directed to that object which is most expedient rather than to objects which enhance the personality at the cost of genuine sacrifice. It differs from authentic ethical choice because an ethical choice is directed not to immediate gains but to what Kierkegaard refers to as man's own eternal validity. By this he means that the ethical personality realizes that he is more than just a prey to the alternative choices which beckon man to various immediate fulfillments. Man, in choosing ethically, chooses himself because he realizes that he is more than a merely sensuous being who lives for the moment. What is important to the ethical personality is the

---

[1] Kierkegaard uses the term "existent" in his works to stress the fact that logic prescinds from, and is indifferent to, human existence (which is characterized by choice, becoming). See Walter Lowrie's introduction to the Postscript, XVIII.

[2] Søren Kierkegaard, Either-Or, Vol. II, Trans by Walter Lowrie (New York: Doubleday & Co., Inc., 1959), p. 171.

inward struggle to achieve authentic selfhood rather than momentary and superficial satisfactions:

> The constant intercourse with the world-historical tends in fact to make the individual unfit for action. The true ethical enthusiast consists in willing to the utmost limits of one's powers, but at the same time being so uplifted in divine jest as never to think about the accomplishment. As soon as the will begins to look right and left for results, the individual begins to become immoral....A truly great ethical personality would seek to realize his life in the following manner. He would strive to develop himself with the utmost exertion of his powers; in so doing he would perhaps produce great effects in the external world. But this would not seriously engage his attention for he would know that the external result is not in his power, and hence that it has no significance for him either pro or contra.[1]

Kierkegaard, speaking as Judge Williams, is admitting that the aesthetic personality does choose in some sense. He does not, however, choose his eternal validity, i.e., himself, as a choosing being, whose choices fulfill the self. What are those choices?

> Duty is the universal, what is required of me is the universal; what I am able to do is the particular....Here personality is displayed in its highest validity. It is not lawless, neither does it make laws for itself. For the definition of duty holds good, but personality reveals itself as the unity of the universal and the particular.[2]

---

[1] Søren Kierkegaard, <u>Concluding Unscientific Postscript</u>, trans. David F. Swenson. Completed after his death by Walter Lowrie (Princeton: Princeton University Press, 1968) p. 121.

[2] Kierkegaard, <u>Either-Or</u>, p. 268.

The ethical personality appropriates to itself the universal. Duty in a closely paralleled Kantian sense is what Kierkegaard is advocating through the person of Judge William in <u>Either-Or</u> with an important exception: for Kierkegaard, duty is closely aligned with passion. One chooses that which is universal with passion because it is that which is most important to him as an authentic ethical personality. Passion and universal duty are joined in the individual to produce the highest level of subjectiveness.

In <u>Concluding Unscientific Postscript</u>,[1] Kierkegaard depicts a higher level of existence, Religiousness A, which is presented as an intermediate step between the ethical and Christian levels of existence. Kierkegaard, through Johannes Climacus, says that Religiousness A, which is the religious response of the ethical person who realizes that the attempt to perform continuously one's ethical duties will fail and that one must find God within by a resignation of all finite efforts, is a necessary step to Religiousness B, the Christian level. As Henry Allison says concerning this level:

> The necessity of this advance for the spiritual development of the individual is demonstrated by means of a further comparison of the Socratic and Christian forms of religiousness, here entitled A and B, or the "religiousness of immanence" and "paradoxical religiousness" respectively. The former is characterized by a "dying away of immediacy," the repudiation,

---

[1] In the title the word "concluding" refers to Kierkegaard's original intention to terminate his literary work. (See Walter Lowrie's introduction to the <u>Postscript</u>.) After the <u>Postscript</u> (1846), Kierkegaard entered upon the production of the works under his own name which are religious in nature. I identify the <u>Postscript</u> as "aesthetic" in that: (1) he still uses a pseudonym (Johannes Climacus) and (2) it is an expression of how a non-Christian looks upon Christianity (Climacus), not how Kierkegaard himself actually views it (which can be accurately determined only by an assessment of his religious works).

or at least relativization of all one's finite concerns, and the devotion of all one's energies to the realization of one's "absolute telos," a phrase applied to both the individual's God-relationship and his eternal happiness, which seem to be identical for Climacus. Since the presupposition of this level of inwardness is the belief that the truth lies within, the individual is viewed as already potentially in possession of his God-relationship or eternal happiness, and his task is simply to transform his mode of existence so as to become in truth what he already is potentially. Hence, Climacus calls this level the 'dialectic of inward transformation."[1]

Kierkegaard considers all these three levels of existence in some way continuous. His notions of inwardness and passion are drawn with the aid of the stages of existence. No one is purely at one level or another. The ethical individual has not abrogated his aesthetic life but has put choices of expediency into their proper perspective. Likewise, those who are at the level of Religiousness A are not of a type which precludes the aesthetic and ethical. And when Kierkegaard does allude to Christian faith, as in Either-Or, the notion of the continuity between the ethical and religious levels is apparent. Judge William, the advocate of the ethical life in Either-Or, Vol II, sees the ethical life as intimately involved with religious factors. This relationship is aptly summarized:

> Strangely, ethical choices indicate two kinds of movement, free self-development and obedient fulfillment of divine purpose. First, the person is realized only by his own self-determination. Self-identity comes into

---

[1] Henry E. Allison, "Christianity and Nonsense", Essays on Kierkegaard, ed. by Jerry H. Gill, (Minneapolis: Burgess Publishing Co., 1969), pp. 136-137.

existence by the very act of choice. Second, the self which is chosen does somehow already exist, for a person does not create himself but only chooses himself. He repents himself back into himself, back into the family, into the race, until he finds himself in God. Becoming oneself is thus both an admission of sin and a rejection of sin.[1]

For Kierkegaard, in his aesthetic works, the levels of existence are mainly presented as a matter of priority, not exclusion.

Yet despite this fact, there are many passages in the aesthetic works where Kierkegaard speaks of Christian faith as a radical departure from such a continuity. The reasonableness of both the aesthetic and ethical levels can be argued as Kierkegaard himself does in <u>Either-Or</u>.[2]

But at times, he depicts Christian faith in an entirely different manner. It is not only objectively uncertain, but is absurd. In <u>Concluding Unscientific Postscript</u>, Kierkegaard says:

> In so far as the absurd comprehends within itself the factor of becoming, one way of approximation will be that which confuses the absurd fact of such a becoming (which is the object of faith) with a simple historical fact, and hence seeks historical certainty for that which is absurd, because it involves the contradiction that something which can become historical only in direct opposition to all human reason, has become historical.

---

[1] George E. Arbaugh and George B. Arbaugh, <u>Kierkegaard's Authorship</u> (Augustana College Library, 1967), pp. 82-82.

[2] Kierkegaard's argument for the ethical level of existence will be exemplified in Chapter IV.

> It is this contradiction which constitutes the absurd, and which can only be believed.[1]

Kierkegaard speaks in the same work of the paradoxical notion of faith. Whereas Religiousness A posited eternal truth within man, Christian faith precludes any such possibility. Man is in sin. He must thrust himself upon the absurd belief in One Who brings him the truth:

> But if existence has in this manner acquired a power over him, he is prevented from taking himself back into the eternal by way of recollection. If it was paradoxical to posit the eternal truth in relationship to an existing individual, it is now absolutely paradoxical to posit it in relationship to such an individual as we have here defined. But the more difficult it is made for him to take himself out of existence by way of recollection, the more profound is the inwardness that his existence may have in existence; and when it is made impossible for him, when he is held so fast in existence that the back door of recollection is forever closed to him, then his inwardness will be the most profound possible.[2]

It does seem as if Kierkegaard is writing in Concluding Unscientific Postscript for the expressed purpose of generating belief in the Christian paradox because it most intensely accentuates man's subjectivity. One could conclude that belief in the paradox is not so much true as valuable to an eminent degree; man's passion and inwardness are at their highest peak because of such irrational faith:

> As a consequence, the believer's existence is still more passionate than the existence of the Greek philosopher, who needed a high degree of passion even in relation to his ataraxy; for existence generates passion,

---

[1] Kierkegaard, Concluding Unscientific Postscript, pp. 189-190.

[2] Ibid, pp. 186-187.

but existence paradoxically accentuated generates the maximum of passion.[1]

The absurdity of faith, though not Christian faith, is depicted in Fear and Trembling where Kierkegaard, through Johannes de Silentio, presents Abraham's resolve to sacrifice his son Isaac at God's command as a model of irrational faith. Ethical considerations are abrogated in order to attain a religious level of existence. Kierkegaard says, "For the movements of faith must constantly be made by virtue of the absurd...."[2] Abraham represents the hero of faith because "the whole earthly form he exhibits is a new creation by virtue of the absurd."[3]

It is not difficult to understand that on the face of it, eminent philosophers have repudiated Kierkegaard as an irrationalist. Thus Brand Blanshard argues that Kierkegaard's notion of faith is meaningless:

> If we are told that though a certain belief were improbable, we should try to make ourselves believe it, that would be intelligible, whether ethical or not. If we were told that a belief, though beyond our present understanding was vouched for by others who did understand it, and that though provisionally accepting this assurance we might come to understand it ourselves, that too would make sense. But if we are told that although a belief is both unintelligible and self-contradictory, we shall see that it is absolutely true and certain if we commit ourselves to it passionately enough, we can only question whether the proposer knows what he is asking of us. The law of contradiction is not a principle that is valid in some cases and

---

[1] Ibid., p. 316.

[2] Søren Kierkegaard, Fear and Trembling and The Sickness Unto Death, trans. with Introduction and Notes by Walter Lowrie (New York: Doubleday & Co., 1944) p. 48.

[3] Ibid., p. 51.

> not in others; if it is invalid in any case,
> it is invalid as such and therefore in every
> case. But if it is thus universally invalid,
> then in no case does the assertion of some-
> thing as true exclude the truth of its denial,
> and nothing is true rather than untrue.
> And that makes assertion meaningless, for what
> could one be asserting?[1]

Not only does Blanshard see Kierkegaard's exposition of faith as illogical, but he views his depiction of Abraham as a "knight of faith" as an allowance for immorality:

> The Christian saint, we must admit, has at times
> been a strange character whose asceticism and
> other-worldliness have set him apart from the
> run of men and caused him to be regarded with
> uncomprehending wonder. Still, in the main
> he has accepted and exemplified the values
> most prized by his fellows and has been
> honored by them accordingly: he has believed in
> the superiority of love to hate, in the
> relief of human misery, in refusing to count
> his own good as more important than that of
> others. These are virtues that we can see
> to be virtues with our unaided human facul-
> ties. But for Kierkegaard as for Luther, these
> faculties are corrupt; all the principles
> laid down by them are open to a "teleological
> suspension of the ethical" imposed from
> above; they are subject at any moment to
> cancellation by "the absurd"; and if, in the
> face of such a suspension we retain our old
> adherence to love or loyalty or even conscience
> in its natural sense, the charge of immorality
> is compounded with a charge of impiety.[2]

---

[1] Brand Blanshard, "Kierkegaard On Faith", *Essays on Kierkegaard*, ed. by Jerry H. Gill (Minneapolis: Burgess Publishing Co., 1969), pp. 119-120.

[2] Ibid., p. 118.

Does Kierkegaard's use of "paradox" and "absurdity" refer to Kierkegaard's belief that faith is an exception to "the law of contradiction"? These arguments pass muster only if we could agree with Blanshard that one finds in Kierkegaard's writings the type of logical relations which traditional logicians refer to as the "table of opposition." Opposites such as A and O statements are contradictions. If A is true, O must be false, and vice versa. As one philosopher has noted:

> Kierkegaard did not fall into this error of committing or advocating logical paradoxes... He gives no indication that Christianity hinders a person in logical paradoxicality. Indeed, he attacks this type of sloppy thinking.[1]

Kierkegaard's use of paradox, which has led critics such as Blanshard to accuse him of positing faith as illogical, should not, as we shall see, be confused with the notion of logical contradiction in the Aristotelian sense. Kierkegaard uses the notion of paradox to stress the fact that the God-man in history cannot be understood <u>pro</u> or <u>contra</u> (Section B, this Chapter), and more importantly to point out that the true paradox of Christianity is existential (Chapter II). It consists in the opposition between what Christianity demands of existents and the unwillingness of them to respond accordingly. As we shall see when we evaluate Kierkegaard's religious writings, a true assessment of Kierkegaard's meaning of paradox can easily be misconstrued by evaluating his aesthetic works alone. At this juncture, we can at least say that a proper assessment of the paradox question <u>cannot</u> be gleaned from Kierkegaard's aesthetic works. Blanshard's criticism of Kierkegaard as a proponent of illogicality is derived from these works alone. Kierkegaard himself discounts any accurate evaluation of his true thought in them. As he says in a non-aesthetic work concerning Johannes Climacus' deprecation of reason in <u>Concluding Unscientific Postscript</u> and <u>Philosophical Fragments</u>:

---

[1] E. D. Klemke, "Logicality vs. Alogicality", <u>Journal of Religion</u>, Vo. XXXVIII, No. 1 (April, 1958), pp. 107-115.

> Every defense of Christianity which understands what it would accomplish must behave conversely maintaining with might and main by qualitative dialectic that Christianity is implausible.¹

What is Kierkegaard's motive for denigrating reason and openly asserting the implausibility of Christian faith? The "ploy" of Kierkegaard is a result of his disenchantment with those who would identify essential Christianity with doctrine, rather than with a commitment made by those who see themselves as dominated by sin and the Christian message as essentially that which speaks to inauthentic man. Kierkegaard wants to stress the fact that speculation on Christian doctrine is not of the essence of Christian faith. As one author has stated concerning Kierkegaard's efforts in presenting Christian faith as implausible in the <u>Postscript</u>:

> The weight of Christian history adds no element of plausibility for faith, and the eighteen centuries tend only to bathe one in comfortable delusion...Speculation may be able to reflect a doctrine and at that perhaps quite unfavorably, but it cannot evaluate faith.²

---

[1] Søren Kierkegaard, <u>On Authority and Revelation: The Book on Adler: or a Cycle of Ethics-Religions Essays</u>, trans. with Introduction and Notes by Walter Lowrie (New York: Harper and Row, Publishers, 1955), p. 62.

[2] George E. Arbaugh and George B. Arbaugh, <u>Kierkegaard's Authorship</u>, p. 200.

Kierkegaard's notion of paradox is always involved with his depiction of the four levels of existence in the pseudonymous works. But the real either-or, for Kierkegaard, is between aesthetic existence and Religiousness B, Christianity. This is evinced by Kierkegaard's non-pseudonymous works, which present authentic Christian faith vis-à-vis aesthetic, spiritless Christianity. The doctrine of the four levels of existence does not appear in these works. And it is important to note that in the pseudonymous works Kierkegaard is admittedly careless in regard to the number and inter-play of the levels.[1] The doctrine of the levels is a product of the pseudonymous authorship alone and cannot be taken as Kierkegaard's own view. As Kierkegaard himself says:

> I have no opinion about these works except as third person, no knowledge of their meaning except as a reader....I am just as far from being Johannes de Silentio in Fear and Trembling as I am from being the Knight of Faith whom he depicts....[2]

---

[1] The various pseudonyms write at one time as if there were two levels, at another time three, and yet at another, four. Also, the opposition between faith and reason is at one time developed via the contrast between the ethical and religious level, as in Fear and Trembling; at another time, in Concluding Unscientific Postscript, such an opposition appears as the contrast between Religiousness A and Religiousness B.

[2] Søren Kierkegaard, The Point of View For My Works As An Author: A Report to History, ed. with a preface by Benjamin Nelson, trans. with Introduction and Notes by Walter Lowrie (New York: Harper and Row, 1962), p. 39.

Since the charge of Kierkegaard's advocacy of faith as illogical rests upon Kierkegaard's own belief in the doctrine of the levels of existence (i.e. the contrast between the ethical and religious levels in Fear and Trembling, and that between Religiousness A and Religiousness B in Concluding Unscientific Postscript) such a charge seems baseless.[1] Kierkegaard's inconsistencies in regard to his description of the levels of existence and in regard to his viewing the ethical as at one time continuous with the religious level (as in Either-Or) and at another discontinuous (as in Fear and Trembling) now makes sense given Kierkegaard's use of the pseudonyms purely as a device for his own purposes. As Alistair McKinnon says regarding Kierkegaard's supposed irrationalism:

> At least most of the problem disappears when we recognize that the doctrine of the stages was an intellectual framework specifically designed to achieve and promote a particular effect and that it is not taken seriously by Kierkegaard in his private person.[2]

The charge of irrationalism is unsound from another vantage point. Kierkegaard does not once speak of the irrationality of faith in his non-pseudonymous works. Terms such as "paradox" and "absurd" are confined to his aesthetic works:

> The fact that words such as Absurde and Paradoks are confined to the pseudonymous literature surely means that his "irrationalism" (if that is what it is) is itself confined thereto. But, again, those works are not his works, nor are its views his views.

---

[1] This is admittedly a negative response to the charge of illogicality. The carelessness of Kierkegaard's treatment of various notions does not with certainty refute the charge. It should, however, guard us against unfounded criticisms. As my argument develops, the more positive response to that charge should become apparent as I attempt to elucidate Kierkegaard's notion of faith as reasonable.

[2] Alistair McKinnon, "Irrationalism Revisited", International Philosophical Quarterly, Vol. IX, No. 2 (June, 1969), p. 170.

> Instead, as he insisted, it was a deliberately
> contrived artifice addressed to an aesthetic
> generation and calculated to point them in
> the direction of faith. In short, the character-
> istic prominence of these signs of irrationalism
> in the pseudonymous works is a function not of
> Kierkegaard's own position but of the problem
> to which these works are specifically addressed.[1]

What is the "problem" which led Kierkegaard to advance the inconsistencies noted? Kierkegaard is primarily interested in spurring on what he considered aesthetic Christians to look within; there, he believes, is the sole hope for spiritual recovery. Kierkegaard's intent in his aesthetic works is not to speak directly concerning Christian doctrine, but to act as a gadfly, in the manner of Socrates, to those whom Kierkegaard considered inauthentic Christians. In these works, it is the inner, passionate life of individual Christians which is paramount for Kierkegaard, not the reflection upon Christian truth. But Kierkegaard tells us that eventually the more direct method of speaking in Christian categories must supplant his more indirect method of reaching aesthetic existents--hence the contrast between the motive in writing his aesthetic works and that which enticed him to write the religious ones:

> The communication of Christianity must ultimate-
> ly end in "bearing witness", the maieutic form
> can never be final. For truth, from the
> Christian point of view, does not lie in the
> subject (as Socrates understood it), but in a
> revelation which must be proclaimed.
>
> In Christendom the maieutic form can certainly
> be used, simply because the majority in fact
> live under the impression that they are
> Christians. But since Christianity is Christian-
> ity, the maieuticer must become the witness.[2]

---

[1] Ibid., p. 176.

[2] Søren Kierkegaard, The Journals of Kierkegaard, trans., selected and with an introduction by Alexander Dru (New York: Harper & Row, Publishers, 1958), pp. 145-146.

Kierkegaard is directing his appeal--in what he considers the most subtle manner--to aesthetic Christians. He says:

> What does it mean, to "deceive?" It means that one does not begin directly with the matter one wants to communicate, but begins by accepting the other man's illusion as good money. So (to stick to the theme with which this work especially deals) one does not begin thus: I am a Christian; you are not a Christian. Nor does one begin thus: It is Christianity I am proclaiming; and you are living in purely aesthetic categories. No, one begins thus: Let us talk about aestheticism. The deception consists in the fact that one talks thus merely to get to the religious theme. But, on our assumption, the other man is under the illusion that the aesthetic is Christianity; for he thinks I am a Christian, and yet he lives in aesthetic categories.[1]

To charge Kierkegaard with proposing an illogical leap of faith is unsupportable because: (1) as we have seen, Kierkegaard is not dealing with logical contradiction in the Aristoletian sense; (2) the specific way in which he considers Christianity paradoxical can be accurately assessed only in his non-aesthetic works; and (3) as we shall see in Chapter II, his notion of paradox in the non-aesthetic works points to the fact that such a notion refers only to the difficulty with which the will moves in the direction of faith. Thus, it is Kierkegaard's notion of will which must be examined to show in what respect Kierkegaard considers faith reasonable. The leap of faith, for Kierkegaard, is a "leap" only because of the recalcitrance of the will in moving in the direction of faith. Despite the limitations in understanding the doctrines of faith adequately, Kierkegaard believes that if existents come to terms with their inauthentic state, faith as a remedy for that state can be appreciated as a reasonable option. Let us first analyze more closely Kierkegaard's denigration of logic so that we can determine in what restrictive sense he is an enemy of reason.

---

[1] Kierkegaard, The Point of View for My Work as an Author, pp. 40-41.

B. **Faith as Alogical**

Although Kierkegaard's repudiation of the aesthetic works is representative of his own view, he admits that there are indications in these works of what would follow in his religious works under his own authorship. Thus he says:

> Anyone who considers the aesthetic work as the whole and then considers the religious part from this point of view, could only consider it as a falling away, a falling off. I have shown in the foregoing that the assumption upon which this point of view is based is not tenable. Thus it was established that from the very beginning, and simultaneously with the pseudonymous work, certain signals, displaying my name, gave telegraphic notice of the religious.[1]

What "telegraphic notice" has he given us regarding the precise manner in which faith is <u>not</u> rational? For Kierkegaard, an individual does not become aware of essential Christianity by philosophical and/or historical arguments. This is the meaning of Kierkegaard's inveighing against all efforts to present it as merely another body of knowledge to be weighed as true or false by the criteria adopted in such areas. As Kierkegaard says concerning the apologetic efforts of his day:

> If one were to describe the whole orthodox apologetic effort in one single sentence, but also with categorical precision, one might say that it has the intent to make <u>Christianity plausible</u>. To this one might add that if this were to succeed, then would this effort have the ironical fate that precisely upon the day of its triumph it would have lost everything and entirely quashed Christianity.[2]

It is not that Kierkegaard sees apologetic efforts as entirely irrelevant, but they are, for him, not primary. The study of Christianity is preliminary to the more essential part of personal conviction and commitment:

---

[1] Ibid., p. 39.
[2] Søren Kierkegaard, <u>On Authority and Revelation,</u> p. 59.

> Reasons do not motivate conviction; conviction motivates the reasons. All that went before was merely preparatory study, something preliminary, something that will disappear as soon as conviction makes is appearance and transforms everything, or turns the relationship around. Otherwise there would not be any repose in a conviction either; for then having a conviction would mean constantly repeating lessons to prove it.[1]

Kierkegaard's denigration of reason in his aesthetic works is not an admission on his part that faith is illogical but a device to make nominal Christians aware of what essential Christianity is, and what it isn't. Understanding and appreciating the Christian faith are necessary but not sufficient conditions of authentic Christian living. And no amount of historical and logical analysis will lead to any firm conclusion concerning the Incarnation. Faith in this sense is alogical. It is acting upon the understanding that Kierkegaard feels aesthetic Christians already have that is the essence of Christian growth. That is the meaning of what Kierkegaard says in his religious work, <u>For Self Examination</u>:

> Therefore, we men, cunning as we always are in relation to God and godly truth, have concentrated our whole attention upon understanding and knowing; we pretend that it is here the difficulty lies, and that then the consequence naturally follows that if only we understood what is right, it then follows as a matter of course that we would do it. Oh, tragic misunderstanding, or cunning invention! No, infinitely farther than from the profoundest ignorance to the clearest understanding to doing accordingly what human and worldly shrewdness teaches the initiated--is that to come to oneself? Yes, according to the opinion of the merely human view. But not according to the Christian opinion; for this is not to come to oneself, it is to come to

---

[1] <u>The Diary of Søren Kierkegaard</u>, ed. by Peter P. Rohde, trans. by Gerda M. Anderson, (New York: Philosophical Library, 1960), p. 165.

the probable; on that road one never gets any farther.[1]

In <u>Concluding Unscientific Postscript</u>, Kierkegaard, through Johannes Climacus, displays the fear he has of Christianity being identified with any logical system. But the aesthetic works are not to be considered as evidence of his own views. Kierkegaard presents Climacus as attacking logic and speculative thought for denigrating subjectivity, passion and inwardness as factors which are good in themselves. Climacus, however, fails to specify how these factors are truly related to Christian faith. (I hope to clarify the nexus between them in the chapter to follow and relate that connection to Kierkegaard's view of faith as reasonable.) For Climacus, an existential system is not possible because existence is movement and change while a logical system is purely static; he condemns the confusion of logic with metaphysics. As James Collins says regarding Kierkegaard's treatment of the relationship between act and potency, thought and existence:

> Becoming, along with the principles of act and potency which are involved in becoming is withdrawn from the existential sphere. The ideas of becoming, act, and potency, are taken by themselves and hypostatized. Their reference to empirically real conditions is rejected, in favor of a "pure" treatment in terms of separate essences, which are no longer referred either to real eternity or to real existence. The result is to endow the dialectical method with a pseudo sort of necessity and to view things under a specious form of eternity, which refuses to acknowledge itself as dependent upon an empirical, abstractive act of the human mind. Pure thought views changing things in the light of a false notion of being and eternity, replacing real change by a dialectical play upon the idea of becoming. Systematic

---

[1] Kierkegaard, <u>For Self-Examination and Judge For Yourselves</u>, trans. by Walter Lowrie, (Princeton: Princeton University Press, 1944), p. 134.

thought is in complete antithesis to God's way of knowing and including the world of temporal existence. He gives to existents their to be, which is a becoming whereas the System revokes the very conditions which alone permit of real becoming.¹

Logical arguments and/or statements simply are, while existing man is becoming:

> The transition from possibility to actuality is, as Aristotle rightly says, a kinesis, a movement. This cannot be expressed or understood in the language of abstraction; for in the sphere of the abstract, movement cannot have assigned to it either time or space which presuppose movement or are pre-supposed by it. Here then there is a pause, and a leap. If someone were to say that this seems to be so only because I think about some definite thing and fail to abstract; that if I did abstract I would perceive that there is no breach of continuity,--my reiterated answer would be that this is quite correct,that from the abstract point of view there is no breach of continuity. But neither is there any movement, since from this point of view everything is.²

Kierkegaard, through Climacus, is explaining the infinite distance that separates the thinker, per se, from the existent who chooses and acts in the moral sphere. Thought is identified with the possible, reality with the actual. By possible, Kierkegaard means the non-actual, that which attempts to appropriate the actual but never can because it is merely thought. The deprecation of reasoning in this context is to be construed as Kierkegaard's attempt to admonish his readers that any identification of true Christianity with any logical system is

---

¹ James Collins, The Mind of Kierkegaard (The Illinois: Henry Regnery Co., 1967), pp. 132-3.

² Kierkegaard, Concluding Unscientific Postscript, p.306.

erroneous. But Kierkegaard is interested in applying his analysis only to the moral sphere. Abstraction has its place, e.g., mathematics, science, philosophy, etc., but it can never identify itself with the moral struggle that <u>actually</u> takes place within the individual. This is what Kierkegaard means when he says:

> The way of objective reflection leads to abstract thought, to mathematics, to historical knowledge of different kinds, and always it leads away from the subject, whose existence or non-existence, and from the objective point of view quite rightly, becomes infinitely indifferent....And yet, the objectivity which has thus come into being is, from the subjective point of view, at the most, either an hypothesis or an approximation, because all eternal decisiveness is rooted in subjectivity.[1]

Thus, Kierkegaard is condemning logic and objective reflection only as a total account of being. Science and philosophy must use the tools of abstract thought; Kierkegaard himself must use it to show its misuse. But pure reflection cannot adequately conceptualize the man who must choose in religious areas. What abstraction does when it attempts to completely identify itself with such dynamic movement is to nullify that which it is attempting to capture. For all its legitimacy, it is lost. Kierkegaard argues that because man's moral life is essentially rooted in immediate choice, it is impossible adequately to conceptualize it. Speculation can never "get at" choice because it is always one step "behind" this existential reality. It can never have a beginning in this reality because it deals with the possible and the static, while religious choices are involved with the real and non-conceptualizable decisions of the moral life. Choice, for Kierkegaard, has no time factor. One can think about what to choose for a certain length of time, but the actual choice is not something that can be positioned within any such parameter. The preliminary thought can be analyzed in ways that the choice cannot. This is Kierkegaard's meaning when he says:

---

[1] <u>Ibid.</u>, p. 173.

> How does the System begin with the immediate?
> That is to say, does it begin with it
> immediately? The answer to this question
> must be an unconditional negative. If the
> System is presumed to come after existence,
> by which a confusion with an existential system
> may be occasioned, then the System is of course
> ex post facto, and so does not begin immediately
> with the immediacy with which existence began;
> although in another sense it may be said that
> existence does not begin with the immediate,
> since the immediate never is as such but is
> transcended as soon as it is.[1]

As regards proving the doctrines of Christianity, faith is alogical for Kierkegaard. But, as we shall see, there is a reasonable aspect to faith which pertains to the reasonableness of willing even when no amount of rational inquiry of the doctrines of faith is of avail. This is the only interpretation that is consistent with what Kierkegaard says in both his aesthetic and non-aesthetic works. It is within this context that we should understand all of Kierkegaard's deprecations of reason in his aesthetic works. Kierkegaard's use of such concepts as "paradox" and "absurd" is not an indication of his belief that faith is illogical. To grasp the full meaning of what he asserts pseudonymously in his aesthetic works, we must again revert to the overall purpose that he himself has set out for us. Kierkegaard's assertion of the paradox of the God-man in history in the aesthetic works is so that the choice of faith can be viewed as the result of seeing it primarily as an alternative to aesthetic living. But one must first recognize oneself as aesthetic before faith can be recognized as such. Thus, Kierkegaard's notion of the paradox is primarily to generate within aesthetic individuals the conviction that true, Christian living begins in individual, passionate self-examination, not merely in examining and digesting the doctrines of the Lutheran faith of his day. The "telegraphic signal" of what would follow in the religious works is that there has been too much stress on speculation concerning faith and not enough on the passionate living of it.

---

[1] Ibid., pp. 101-102.

I have not yet shown how Kierkegaard applies reason to faith, but have paved the way by attempting to prove that the case for Kierkegaard's advocacy of faith as illogical is not well-founded, and that he is in actuality attacking those who would identify logic and speculation with authentic Christianity. The above are interpretations which are consistent with his religious and aesthetic works, especially in light of a proper understanding of the functions of the aesthetic works, the obvious laxity with which he depicts the levels of existence, and the inconsistencies in his use of such notions as paradox and absurd.

Kierkegaard's argument for faith cannot be of the formal, apologetic type. (As I have indicated, Kierkegaard sees this as a prerequisite for faith, not as a sufficient condition of it). I shall attempt to show in the following chapters that his is an argument which will advance the case for the reasonableness of willing for faith in Christ instead of the continuation of the sterile kind of faith which Kierkegaard feels exists in the Christianity of his day.

CHAPTER II

KIERKEGAARD'S PSYCHOLOGICAL WORKS

The sense in which Kierkegaard considers faith reasonable must initially be gleaned from his non-aesthetic works. In this chapter I will attempt to show how his notions of dread and despair refer to what Kierkegaard thinks is a major obstacle to an authentic faith in Christ. I will not, however, attempt to evaluate the adequacy of Kierkegaard's psychological thesis. My purpose is to state that thesis and evaluate the importance it had for him in his assessment of faith as reasonable. I shall: (1) present as clearly as possible Kierkegaard's psychological thesis; (2) analyze the notion of will that is derived from such a thesis and show how Kierkegaard considers it to be relevant to the reasonableness of faith; and (3) conclude that Kierkegaard's notions of dread and despair warrant us to state that the actual paradox of faith, for Kierkegaard, refers to an existential paradox that is at the very heart of Kierkegaard's consideration of faith as reasonable.

A. Dread and Despair

Kierkegaard's two great psychological works are Concept of Dread (1844) and Sickness Unto Death (1849). Kierkegaard considered the latter one of his two greatest works and an expression of his deepest psychological discoveries. Since Concept of Dread is very close in style and content to Sickness Unto Death, we can consider this to be an expression of Kierkegaard's own psychological insights despite the use of the pseudonymous author, Vigilius Haufniensis. Unlike the other pseudonymous works written in this period, this one does not attempt to present a dialectical view of the various levels of existence. Kierkegaard is dealing directly with the concepts of dread and sin. He analyzes them in such a way as to leave no impression that he is presenting incomplete truths.[1]

---

[1] In Sickness Unto Death a pseudonym is also used, Anti-Climacus. All of Kierkegaard's later works were intended to be written under his own name. The use of the pseudonym in question was an afterthought and Kierkegaard attempted to have the use of the name deleted from Training in Christianity (1850). Although Kierkegaard failed, he did manage to delete it from For Self Examination (1851). [Walter Lowrie, A Short Life of Kierkegaard (Princeton: Princeton University Press, 1942 p. 217].

In both works, Kierkegaard is analyzing the deepest psychological experiences of man. He begins by describing man as a synthesis of body and soul united by a third element, spirit. It is clear from these works that soul is not an ultimate substance in a Thomistic sense. Activities of the soul, for Kierkegaard, pertain to man's sentient and thinking processes. Spirit is the uniting factor of these two opposing elements. What is spirit? Kierkegaard tells us that spirit is the self, and he equates self with will--the more will, the more self. Yet he wishes to describe man by means of another synthesis: "So then, man was said to be a synthesis of soul and body; but he is at the same time a <u>synthesis of the temporal and the eternal</u>."[1] The very fact that Kierkegaard has presented us with a new synthesis is evidence of the fact that he is not attempting to analyze man in a Cartesian fashion. Instead, he is giving us a description of those activities in man that are clear to him from experience. The first synthesis refers to man's physical as well as mental experiences. Man gains power over himself in bringing these two disparate activities into harmony by means of will. The man who does not decisively will has no real self. Kierkegaard realizes that we are not cognizant of body, soul, and spirit as separate entities. We act and consider ourselves as one. However, we are aware of purely bodily functions as well as those which are sentient and mental (soul). We are also aware that our identity as creatures who experience both of these activities is enhanced by decisiveness. The second synthesis is another attempt on Kierkegaard's part to describe men's nature.

> The synthesis of the eternal and the temporal is not a second synthesis but is the expression for the first synthesis in consequence of which man is synthesis of soul and body sustained by spirit.[2]

Thus Kierkegaard is not contradicting himself when he tells us at one time that there are two syntheses, and at another time, one. He is positing a second synthesis to supplement his first synthesis, but in reality it is merely an expression of the first.

---

[1] Søren Kierkegaard, <u>The Concept of Dread</u>, trans. with introduction and notes by <u>Walter Lowrie</u> (New Jersey: Princeton University Press, 1944), p. 76.

[2] <u>Ibid.</u>, p. 79.

By means of the second synthesis, he is describing man as a finite creature with temporal needs and those that are over and above these particular ones. Man's eternal needs relate to his religious aspirations.

The Concept of Dread is a work which deals with the psychological variations that exist in man before spirit is posited. Although sin is a theological category (and Kierkegaard leaves it to dogmatics to say something concrete concerning it), Kierkegaard believes he has discovered the means by which the experience of sin can be vivified:

> Dread is: 'a qualification of the dreaming spirit' ...The reality of the spirit constantly shows itself in a form which entices its possibility, but it is away as soon as one grasps after it, and it is a nothing which is able only to alarm. More it cannot do so long as it only shows itself. One almost never sees the concept dread dealt with in psychology, and I must therefore call attention to the fact that it is different from fear and similar concepts which refer to something definite, whereas dread is freedom's reality as possibility for possibility. One does not therefore find dread in the beast, precisely for the reason that by nature the beast is not qualified by spirit.[1]

Dread is the realization of the infinite possibilities of freedom and, in this sense, the awareness of nothing. Dread is "a qualification of the dreaming spirit" because the object of alarm is vague, amorphous, nothing, yet everything. Kierkegaard is the first philosopher to recognize the general, almost inexpressible, feeling of anxiety present within a person who anticipates his own freedom. He recognizes that there is a dialectical quality to the psychological experience. We are at the same time lured by the feeling of dread and repulsed by it:

> When we consider the dialectical determinants in dread, it appears that they have precisely the characteristic

---

[1] Ibid., p. 38.

ambiguity of psychology. Dread is a sympathetic antipathy and an antipathetic sympathy. One speaks of a sweet dread, a sweet feeling of apprehension, one speaks of a strange dread, a shrinking dread, etc.[1]

Kierkegaard refers to dread as the expression of the weight of our freedom. Spirit is will which synthesizes the body and soul, and before this synthesis is constituted, before man chooses, he foresees the infinite possibilities of choice. Spirit is related to the infinite in that the will is faced with not this choice or that choice, but with myriad avenues in which it can direct itself. This is why dread is ambiguous. There is a certain fascination to evil in that the will can freely choose it without restraint and as a product of its unique self. There is also a nebulous feeling of guilt assigned to dread, but dread is not real guilt until evil has been posited:

> Thus dread is the dizziness of freedom which occurs when the spirit would posit the synthesis, and freedom then gazes down into its own possibility, grasping at finiteness to sustain itself. In this dizziness freedom succumbs....This again is the overwhelming experience which determines the individual's ambiguous relation, both sympathetic and antipathetic. In dread there is the egoistic infinity of possibility, which does not tempt like a definite choice, but alarms (aengster) and fascinates with its sweet anxiety (Beaengsteles).[2]

Although Kierkegaard analyzed dread as proximate to sin but not sin itself, he analyzes despair as man's state as a result of sin. In contrast to his psychological evaluation of dread, he treats despair as the most advanced stage of the genesis of sin and guilt. Before sin arises there is the experience of dread which allures man to evil choices; then there is the choice of sin which is in itself unanalyzable but attested to by immediate experience; finally there is the state of despair which

---

[1] Ibid.

[2] Ibid., p. 55.

is the resultant of this choice--the attempt of man to will inauthentically, to posit spirit in a way that is not compatible with a true self.

Whereas dread was an experience, Kierkegaard's analysis of despair does not lead us to define it as an experience (although it can be experienced) but rather as the ontological state of the lack of right relationship between soul and body. Before spirit was posited, man had an experience (dread) of the infinite possibility of his freedom. Soul and body had not been synthesized. A real self was to be contracted by choice. Man experienced the feeling of both allurement and repugnance to the possible evil that it was in his power to will. And when evil is willed, a false self is effected. Now it is important to note that, although Kierkegaard does at times speak of sin as if it were individually disparate choices, his emphasis, in the main, is on the aesthetic level of existence that an existent has willed to live continuously. Particular sins are a manifestation of a much deeper choice that is the ground for such acts. Thus sin is not so much particular choices, as a stance we continually take in relation to ourselves and before God. Kierkegaard looks upon despair, then, as the dis-relationship in man because of that stance. One in despair has negated his eternal responsibility before God, related himself to the world and himself as an existent that is a result of his own selfish desires, refused to choose himself as the particular person that God intended him to be. Although we usually do experience the result of this basic choice of an inauthentic life style to some degree, we can be so inured to despair (i.e., the state of not being a real self) that we can eventually become spiritless, unconscious of this spiritual malady. In Sickness Unto Death, Kierkegaard undertakes to describe this state of despair, the experiences we have of it, and the psychological nature of our choices which result in this state. Although sin itself qua choice cannot be analyzed, the life experience of it can be described. What man attempts to do when he posits his will evilly and the condition of man as the result of such a choice are analyzable and afford Kierkegaard an opportunity to render a psychological account of man's inauthenticity.

Despair can be reduced to one form; i.e., despair of willing to be one's own self. Whether our attempt to create a false self is conscious or unconscious, weak or defiant, despair is the result of choosing a self of our own making that is not in harmony with God's will. Man, qua spirit, is related to God. To create a self without relating it to God is to create a false self, and to deny the eternal nature of the self:

> This formula (i.e., that the self is constituted by another) is the expression for the total dependence of the relation (the self namely), the expression for the fact that the self cannot of itself attain and remain in equilibrium and rest by itself, but only by relating itself to that Power which constituted the whole relation. Indeed, so far is it from being true that this second form of despair (despair at willing to be one's own self) denotes only a particular kind of despair, that on the contrary all despair can in the last analysis be reduced to this.[1]

Kierkegaard regards the fact that man feels an uneasiness about his self, yet cannot cure himself, cannot become the self that will effect an ultimate and abiding satisfaction, as an indication that the problem with the self rests elsewhere than with a reassessment and reapportionment of interests and attitudes. If despair were merely a question of not willing to be the self that we are at a particular moment of space and time, then man could alter his choices and life-style to meet the crisis. Kierkegaard feels that the problem goes much deeper. Man seems to have insurmountable difficulty in reaching authentic selfhood. Kierkegaard feels that the problem subsists because we do not relate ourselves to the "Power which constituted this whole relation." Man tries again and again to experience complete authenticity. He fails because all his choices continually relate to the way he aesthetically would like himself to be; he forgets the eternal demand of his being. This is why Kierkegaard calls despair "the sickness unto death." Man cannot get rid of his sense of failure to attain authentic selfhood. An experience abides of having a self that is dying; there is an experience that nags at the heart of man that he is not genuine and is losing touch with the very meaning of his being. And yet there seems to be no end to this constant pressure that is brought to bear on the self:

> It is in this last sense that despair is the sickness unto death, this agonizing contradiction, this sickness in the self,

---

[1] Kierkegaard, <u>Fear and Trembling</u> and <u>Sickness Unto Death</u>, p. 147.

everlastingly to die; to die and yet not to die,
to die the death. For dying means to live to
experience death; and if for a single instant
this experience is possible, it is tantamount
to experiencing it forever. If one might die of
despair as one dies of a sickness, then the
eternal in him, the self, must be capable of
dying in the same sense that the body dies of
sickness. But this is an impossibility; the
dying of despair transforms itself constantly
into a living.[1]

For Kierkegaard, this sickness is the worst malady encountered by man. He cannot get rid of the false self by means of any temporal measure. Despair is literally "self-consuming". The experience of the dis-relationship inherent in the choice of sin goes on and on. Despair cannot be properly attributed to anything external to man. If man is in despair <u>over something</u>, then it is not the despair that Kierkegaard wishes to discuss. This is despair that psychologically can be traced to a particular object, not the despair that is related to the self. But the despair that we sometimes analyze as the despair over a temporary, fixed object is, at heart, and on closer analysis, the ontological malady that Kierkegaard is referring to. When we say, for instance, that a man is in despair over the fact that he did not become Caesar, it is not the fact that he did not become Caesar that bothers him. It is the <u>self</u> which did not become Caesar which bothers him, a self which he cannot suffer to be, so as a result, he would wish to become something else. At bottom this is the refusal of the self to become that particular synthesis of soul and body as willed by God. Many times then the underlying cause of a temporal despair is the condition of the sinner in his refusal to be a real self:

> In a profounder sense it is not the fact that
> he did not become Caesar which is intolerable
> to him, but the self which did not become
> Caesar is the thing that is intolerable; or,

---

[1] <u>Ibid.</u>, p. 151.

more correctly, what is intolerable to him is that he cannot get rid of himself. If he had become Caesar he would have been rid of himself in desperation, but now that he did not become Caesar he cannot in desperation get rid of himself. Essentially he is equally in despair in either case, for he does not possess himself, he is not himself.[1]

Whether he had become Caesar or not, the condition of despair remains. To be a self that the sinner really wishes to be would be his delight, but this cannot be. Each individual is willed by God to be a unique synthesis of soul and body; any other synthesis results in a self that is no genuine self at all. The sinner refuses to be a self not of his own making.

True selfhood is, for Kierkegaard, an impossibility for man to achieve by his unaided will. The alluring aspects of dread, which entice him to will evilly, and the resultant state of despair are, for Kierkegaard, evidence of the need for a spiritual recovery. And we must remember as we attempt to assess Kierkegaard's positing of faith as a reasonable moment that Kierkegaard is directing his appeal to Christians who already have a faith in the Christian doctrine of original sin, but have not, in Kierkegaard's mind, truly appropriated it to themselves except as part of the doctrinal body of Christian truth assimilated in an intellectual, non-passionate manner. Thus, Kierkegaard is primarily interested in The Concept of Dread and Sickness Unto Death in attacking the speculative system of thought which attempts to identify the problem of becoming a Christian with ideology, i.e., doctrine and thought, rather than with the struggle within individuals to attain their eternal destiny:

> But to be entirely consistent Speculation must also say, "The thing of being an individual sinner, that's not to be anything, it is subsumed under the concept, waste no time on it etc." And then what further? Is one perhaps to think sin instead of being an individual sinner?--just as one was exhorted to think

---

[1] Ibid., p. 152.

> the concept of man instead of being the
> individual man. And then what further?
> Does a man become himself "sin" by think-
> ing sin? <u>Cogito ergo sum</u>. A capital pro-
> posal! However, one does not even in this
> case need to be afraid of becoming sin...
> the pure sin, for sin cannot be thought.
> This after all Speculation itself must con-
> cede, since sin is in fact a falling away
> from the concept.[1]

Sin is "a falling away from the concept," but Kierkegaard leaves us no doubt that he feels it is more vividly experienced than anything conceptual. No thought can subsume the reality of sin. An individual alone, as spirit, experiences his own inauthenticity. Philosophy has failed to point this out and has treated despair as any other problem:

> In the works of some of the pseudonyms it has
> been shown that in recent philosophy confusion
> has been wrought by talking about doubt when
> one ought to speak of despair...Modern philoso-
> phy, being abstract, hovers in metaphysical
> indefiniteness. Instead then of expounding
> this fact about itself, and thus directing
> men (the individual men) to the ethical,
> the religious, the existential, philosophy
> has made it appear as if men could (as some-
> one has said with blunt honesty) speculate
> themselves out of their own good skin (<u>Skind</u>)
> and into the pure appearance (Skin).[2]

Kierkegaard believes that only by directing aesthetic Christians to their inner, spiritual struggle i.e., dread

---

[1] Kierkegaard, <u>Fear and Trembling</u> and <u>Sickness Unto Death</u> p. 250.

[2] Søren Kierkegaard, <u>Training in Christianity</u>, p. 83.

and despair, can they begin to grasp the essential reasons for believing in Christ. That is why he so maligns any attempt to reach such existents by logical persuasion alone:

> One sees now how extraordinarily (that there might be something extraordinary left)--how extraordinarily stupid it is to defend Christianity, how little knowledge of men this betrays, and how truly even though it be unconsciously, it is working in collusion with the enemy, by making of Christianity a miserable something or another which in the end has to be rescued by a defense. Therefore, it is certain and true that he who first invented the notion of defending Christianity in Christiandom is de facto Judas No. 2; he also betrays with a kiss, only his treachery is that of stupidity.[1]

Although we have briefly alluded to Kierkegaard's notion of will in respect to his attacks on speculative reasoning (Chapter I) and his analysis of despair in this chapter, a more detailed analysis is required in order to assess further Kierkegaard's primary aim as an attempt to persuade aesthetic Christians to come to grips with their inauthentic state and to view faith as a reasonable option to remedy that spiritual malady.

B. <u>Kierkegaard's Concept of Will</u>

Kierkegaard believes aesthetic Christians are powerless to will a change in their inauthentic state. He considers despair nearly universal--all are in despair except those who have lived at the highest level of existence and who have given themselves completely to Christ in faith. For Kierkegaard, an honest assessment of self leads inevitably to the experience of inauthenticity i.e., sin. The paradoxical nature of man, his eternal and temporal needs, are not easily synthesized.

> On the other hand, the ordinary view of despair remains content with appearances, and so it is a superficial view, that is, no view at all. It assumes that every man must know by himself better than anyone

---

[1] Ibid., pp. 217-218.

else whether he is in despair or not. So whoever says that he is in despair is regarded as being in despair, but whoever thinks he is not in despair is not so regarded. Consequently despair becomes a rather rare phenomenon, whereas in fact it is quite universal. It is not a rare exception that one is in despair; no, the rare, the very rare exception is that one is not in despair.[1]

One could interpret Kierkegaard's description of man's precarious spiritual condition as the reason for his belief in a leap of faith. And it is also appropriate that his notion of choice <u>qua</u> choice should be construed as inexplicable, unanalyzable. But for Kierkegaard, the unanalyzable is not the unknowable. Let us then assess Kierkegaard's precise notion of will.

Dread is the concept which Kierkegaard uses to describe sin, but sin <u>qua</u> choice is a sudden and unanalyzable change. And sin is not a state, but a given with which we are all too familiar:

> If sin is dealt with in psychology, the mood becomes the persistence of observation, the dauntlessness of the spy, not the ardent flight of seriousness away from and out of sin. The concept becomes a different one, for sin becomes a state. But sin is not a state. Its idea is that its concept is constantly annulled. As a state (<u>de potentia</u>) it is not, whereas <u>de actu</u> or <u>in actu</u> it is and is again. The mood of psychology would be antipathetic curiosity, but the correct mood is the stouthearted opposition of seriousness. The mood of psychology is the dread corresponding to its discovery, and in its dread it delineates sin, while again and again it is alarmed by the sketch it produces. When sin is treated in such a way it becomes the stronger: for psychology is really related to it in a feminine way. Doubtless there is

---

[1] Søren Kierkegaard, <u>Fear and Trembling</u> and <u>Sickness Unto Death</u>, p. 155.

an element of truth in this state of mind,
and doubtless it emerges in every man's life
more or less before the ethical makes its
appearance; but by such treatment sin
becomes not what it is but more or less than
it is.[1]

Regarding sin, Kierkegaard says that "as a state (de potentia) it is not" because for him sin has no essence. We cannot say that it has this property and that. It just is. The most we can say is that it is an act of will and in this sense it is de actu and in actu again and again. We do experience sin in our individual lives. The best that psychology can do, however, is to try to understand sin by means of the notion of dread that precedes it. Most psychology would attempt to deal with it in an "antipathetic curiosity" or objectivity. This is the "feminine" way in that such a study cannot recognize the horror of sin. The dread with which we are all familiar, that anticipates sin, is closer to sin's reality. Treating sin in a purely behavioristic manner i.e., sin as abnormality, as disharmony, etc., must fall short for "by such a treatment sin becomes not what it is but more or less than it is."[2]

Through his notion of sin, then, Kierkegaard describes choice as transcedent in that it is beyond man's power to conceptualize. He says:

> Every science has its province either in
> immanent logic, or in an immanence within
> a transcedence, that discrimen rerum by
> which sin enters the world, and never has
> it entered otherwise.[3]

There is no science of sin because although sin is an "immanence" in that it is happening within man, it is at the same time transcendent, i.e., outside man's power to analyze. An act of will is experienced, but we cannot conceptualize it. No free act can be explained as a simple consequence of a previous state. Thus,

---

[1] Søren Kierkegaard, The Concept of Dread, p. 14.

[2] Ibid.

[3] Ibid., p. 15.

when Kierkegaard refers to a "leap of faith", he is not implying that such a choice is meaningless; rather he is emphasizing the fact that man's moral life is marked by discontinuity. Innocence to sin, and sin to repentence, are not quantitative changes within an individual; they are qualitative changes:

> Now again psychology has dread as the object of its study, but it must be cautious. The history of the individual life goes forward in a movement from state to state. Every state is posited by a leap. In this way sin came into the world, and so does it continue to come, unless it is stopped. Yet every repetition of it is not a simple consequence but a new leap. Every such leap is preceded by a state, which is the closest approximation to the leap psychology can attain.[1]

But Kierkegaard's emphasis on the fact that sin <u>qua</u> choice is irreducible to analysis by logic and speculative thought, and that the change from the condition of sin to repentance (the leap of faith) and vice versa is the result of a drastic change of will, does not refer to Kierkegaard's belief that choice is an isolated unique event in the existent's life. Kierkegaard speaks of sin not as a particular choice, but as an unwillingness to change one's moral position. He is criticizing the naive attitude of looking upon sin as that which we committed every three or four days. One does not essentially so much commit sin, but allows it to abide by not altering the deeply rooted choice of living aesthetically. A deeper insight into despair is that it is the result of <u>not</u> willing to heal the spiritual recalcitrance which results in the refusal to seek an authentic self. Thus, despair is the condition resulting from a will which will not veer from the continuum of sin. In this context sin <u>is</u> analyzable, although <u>qua</u> choice, it is not:

> The merely desultory way of conceiving the case, which has regard only to the new sin and passes over the intermediate state, the interval between the particular sins, is just as superficial a way of conceiving it as it would be to assume that the railway train moved only when the locomotive puffed. No, this puffing and the onrush

---

[1] <u>Ibid</u>., p. 100.

which succeeds it is really not the thing that
has to be considered, but rather the even
momentum which occasions the puffing.
And so it is with sin. The state of remaining
in sin is in the deepest sense sin, the particular sins are not the continuation of sin, but
they are the expression for the continuation
of sin; in the particular new sins the momentum of sin merely becomes more observable.[1]

Kierkegaard maintains that an existent moves not from choice to choice as if each choice were isolated from the next, but in a predictable manner and only rarely unpredictably. Particular sins are evidence of a style of life the existent has already willed for himself, and continues to will; to will continuously in the same way is the norm. The "leap", admittedly an unusual and difficult choice, is from one kind of moral existence to another. It is a decision not only to make such a transition, but to continuously sustain that change. And Kierkegaard believes that he can reason with aesthetic existents regarding their state, although no analysis of sin and repentance qua choices can be effected. Kierkegaard's emphasis on will rather than intelligence does not mean that Kierkegaard does not think a certain kind of reasoning is effective. In actuality, Kierkegaard believes that sin is the result of a conscious willed action; that our rationalizations about sin are the result of a willed blocking of the understanding; that aesthetic existents knows all too well the growing guilt that they have regarding their state cannot be so easily dispelled:

> That is to say, even if sin be ignorance (or what Christianity would perhaps prefer to call stupidity), which in one sense cannot be denied, we have to ask, is this an original ignorance, is it always the case that one has not known and hitherto could not know anything about the truth, or is it superinduced, a subsequent ignorance? If it is what the last question implies, then sin must properly have its ground in something else, it

---

[1] Søren Kierkegaard, Fear and Trembling and The Sickness Unto Death, p. 237.

> must have its ground in the activity with
> which a man has labored to obscure his
> intelligence.[1]

It is obvious that Kierkegaard feels he knows quite well the trappings of sin and the relationship between will and understanding in regard to the genesis and growth of sin:

> And next comes the question how the will
> likes this thing that is known. If it does
> not like it, it does not follow that the
> will goes ahead and does the opposite of
> that which the intelligence understood,
> such contrasts occur doubltless rather
> seldom; but the will lets some time pass,
> there is an interim, that means, "We'll
> see about that tomorrow." All this while
> the intelligence becomes more and more
> obscure, and the lower nature triumphs
> more and more...The will has no particular
> objection to it--so it says with its fingers
> crossed. And then when the intelligence
> has become duly darkened, the intelligence
> and the will can understand one another
> better; at last they agree entirely, for
> the intelligence has gone over to the side
> of the will and acknowledges that the
> thing is quite right as it would have it.[2]

The important point to be made is that Kierkegaard does not feel that the aesthetic condition of nominal Christians cannot be dealt with in some manner. Although sin cannot be analyzed, it can be best <u>talked about</u> by personal appropriation, and the notion of dread is the best medium through which we can allude to sin:

> Sin does not properly belong in any science.
> It is the theme with which the sermon deals,
> where the individual talks as an individual
> to an individual. In our age scientific self-
> importance has turned the priests into pro-
> fessional parish-clerks of a sort, who also
> serve science and think it beneath their dignity
> to preach. It is no wonder, therefore, that

---

[1] <u>Ibid.</u>, p. 219.

[2] <u>Ibid.</u>, pp. 224-5.

> preaching has come to be regarded as a pretty poor art. Nevertheless, preaching is the most difficult of all arts, and essentially is the art which Socrates extols: the art of being able to converse. From this of course it does not follow that there must be someone in the congregation to make answer, or that it might be a help to have someone regularly introduced to speak. When Socrates censured the Sophists by making the distinction that they were able to talk but not to converse, what he really meant was that they were able to say a great deal about everything, but lacked the factor of personal appropriation. Appropriation is precisely the secret of conversation.[1]

Appropriation is the ability to conjure up in a person the awareness of an inner experience. This cannot be done directly because we are not dealing with an objective truth outside the self; we are dealing with a truth that is common to all, but at the same time individual and not within the power of pure thought to comprehend. Sin can be best dealt with by approaching the subject indirectly, alluding to those experiences which can help the listener focus on the particular experience which it is impossible to understand and analyze directly. Therefore, Kierkegaard feels that all attempts to speak of sin in a completely objective fashion are bound to fail. They will fail because the proper mood is lacking. Dread is the means of appropriation by means of which the individual recognizes the import of sin:

> As soon therefore, as one sees the problem of sin treated, it is possible at once to see from the mood whether the concept is the right one. As so soon as sin is talked about as a sickness, an abnormality, a poison, a disharmony, then the concept too is falsified.[2]

---

[1] Søren Kierkegaard, The Concept of Dread, pp. 14-15.

[2] Ibid., p. 14.

Kierkegaard considers the modern world guilty of viewing sin in a cold, dispassionate, and hence, spurious manner. Modern philosophy talks of sin as "egoism." But such a term is a general category which cannot elucidate the individual, incommunicable experience of sin:

> Seeing that in modern philosophy sin has so often been explained as egoism, it is incomprehensible that no one has perceived that precisely in this consists the impossibility of finding a place for sin in any science. For the egoistic is precisely the particular (Enkelte) and only the particular individual can know it, as a particular individual, since when viewed under general categories it can signify everything, in such wise that this everything signifies nothing at all. Therefore, the definition of sin as egoism may be quite correct, precisely when at the same time one holds fast the fact that, scientifically speaking, it is so empty of content that it means nothing at all.[1]

Because Kierkegaard feels that sin cannot be dealt with in a scientific fashion does not mean that sin cannot be alluded to indirectly. In the same manner it does not mean that one cannot reason with aesthetic existents to persuade them of the beneficial motives in effecting a real change in their lives. This indirect approach was just the vehicle Kierkegaard took in attempting to cajole them to make that change. The precise nature of that indirect type of reasoning that Kierkegaard took will become clearer by an analysis of some of his religious works in Chapter III and his real use of the notion of subjectivity in Chapter IV. It is sufficient to say at this juncture that, in Kierkegaard's mind, not only is his notion of will compatible with an attempt to reason with the aesthetic Christians of his day, but that it is the will to which he must address his appeal. Kierkegaard feels the imperceptible way in which the will delays in following the intellect, and then finally rebels, forces him to attempt to convince aesthetic Christians of the reasonableness of a religious response by means of the unique approach he took in his aesthetic works. His psychological works attest to Kierkegaard's belief that aesthetic existents must first come to terms with their inauthentic state before faith can begin to appear as a reasonable option

---

[1] Ibid., p. 69.

to remedy it. Dread and despair are notions which Kierkegaard uses to describe the insurmountable difficulties of coping with the rebellious character of a will directed to aesthetic interests:

> Sin does not consist in the fact that man has not understood what is right, but in the fact that he will not understand it, and in the fact that he will not do it.[1]

C. Christianity--An Existential Paradox

Kierkegaard feels that if aesthetic existents do see themselves as aesthetic, then the movement of faith will be a reasonable alternative to the continuation in that inauthentic state. At the end of Sickness Unto Death, Kierkegaard says:

> The believer possesses the eternally certain antidote to despair, viz. possibility; for with God all things are possible every instant. This is the sound health of faith which resolves contradictions. The contradiction in this case is that, humanly speaking, destruction is certain, and that nevertheless there is possibility.[2]

Kierkegaard's explication of the notion of possibility in Concept of Dread attests to a different meaning of that concept but one which relates to the same problem. He must not only make individuals aware that faith is "the eternally certain antidote to despair", but also instill in aesthetic existents the belief that they cannot begin to become aware of the spiritual problem at hand until they become cognizant of the dire consequences of dread. Only those who are aware of the myriad possibilities in inauthentic choices can realize that faith is the necessary antidote to spiritual ruin:

> No, in possibility everything is possible, and he who truly was brought up by possibility has comprehended the dreadful as well as the smiling. When such a person, therefore, goes out from the school

---

[1] Kierkegaard, Fear and Trembling and Sickness Unto Death, pp. 225-226.
[2] Ibid., p. 173.

> of possibility, and knows more thoroughly
> than a child knows the alphabet that he
> can demand of life absolutely nothing, and
> that terror, perdition annihilation, dwell
> next door to every man, and has learned
> the profitable lesson that every dread
> which alarms (aengste) may the next instant
> become a fact, he will then interpret reality
> differently, he will extol reality, and even
> when it rests upon him heavily he will remember
> that after all it is far, far lighter
> than the possibility was.[1]

The individual completely enveloped by aesthetic interests has no such dread. Thus, it is only the man filled with dread, not of finite things, but of the possibility of his freedom, who can attain authenticity by seeking security against its terrible possibilities. This is why Kierkegaard says, "If a man were a beast or an angel, he would not be able to be in dread. Since he is a synthesis he can be in dread, and the greater the dread, the greater the man."[2] A man who intensely experiences dread is closer to faith than an individual who does not heed whatever dread exists in him:

> When the discoveries of possibility are
> honestly administered, possibility will
> then disclose all finitudes but idealize
> them in the form of infinity, and by
> dread overwhelm the individual, until he
> in turn conquers them by the anticipation
> of faith.[3]

It is within this context that Kierkegaard refers to Christianity as being in some sense contradictory in his non-aesthetic works. His aesthetic works referred to paradox as an offense to the intellect and we saw that his motive in doing so was to combat nominal Christianity. But the real contradiction essential to Christianity is within the heart of aesthetic existents--the difficulty in overcoming the tendency to allow dread and despair to overpower them. As Kierkegaard says in his non-aesthetic work, <u>Training in Christianity</u>:

---

[1] Søren Kierkegaard, <u>The Concept of Dread</u>, p. 140.

[2] <u>Ibid</u>., p. 139.

[3] <u>Ibid</u>., p. 85.

> But at the absolute the understanding stands still. The contradiction which arrests it is that a man is required to make the greatest possible sacrifice, to dedicate his whole life as a sacrifice....[1]

The lack of aesthetic existents' coming to terms with themselves (making "the greatest possible sacrifice" by changing the direction of their lives, foregoing aesthetic interests and seeing themselves as inauthentic) is the real paradox of Christianity as far as Kierkegaard is concerned. The ill effects of dread and despair which constitute an aesthetic existent's life as contrasted with the spiritual direction he should be taking is, for Kierkegaard, the real contradiction of faith. As N. H. Søe argues concerning Kierkegaard's real notion of paradox:

> Another extremely important point can be expressed in a slightly different way: In Philosophical Fragments it is asserted that the Incarnation "is a folly to the understanding and an offense to the human heart"....that this remark should occur in this particular work is astonishing and therefore worthy of attention.[2]

Søe's point is that in a pseudonymous work, where Kierkegaard is mainly attacking speculation and abstract thought, it is "astonishing" that Kierkegaard would refer to offense in this way unless it were his own thought. E. D. Klemke agrees when he argues:

> To the degree that I become interested in the Christian appeal, I may have to give up all. Jesus Christ is not added to my normal values and ends. For me to be a Christian, says Kierkegaard, may mean that I will have to give up all interests and goals in order to follow Christ. Thus, no one is a Christian by first birth. One must become an unconditional

---

[1] Søren Kierkegaard, Training in Christianity and the Edifying Discourse Which Accompanied It, trans. with introduction and notes by Walter Lowrie (Princeton: Princeton University Press, 1941), p. 121.

[2] N. H. Søe, "Kierkegaard's Doctrine of the Paradox", A Kierkegaard Critique, Edited by Howard A. Johnson and Niels Thulstrup (New York: Harper and Brothers, 1962), p. 216.

believer, whereby he is willing to give up all
personal conditions and preferences. Then the
behavioral paradoxicality disappears, not
permanently, but in moments and hours, as life
keeps fluctuating.[1]

Klemke does not negate, for Kierkegaard, the importance of reflection for the would-be believer, but it is not understanding which can ever be the crucial factor in the movement of faith--one must put understanding into practice. It is a resolution of despair that is paramount, not an assessment of Christianity in its doctrinal form; aesthetic existents too well hide the need for such a resolution:

What keeps men from faithing (I use "faithing"
rather than "believing" to distinguish the non-
cognitive from the cognitive function)?
Kierkegaard has done much to trace this to the
lack of a need for faithing, which is hidden
from people because of the illusions which
cover the need. When the passions in which
people place their faith are destroyed, one of
the central tasks of Christianity, then, is to
take away illusions from people so that the
need for faith may arise. As long as men live
under these illusions or believe that they can
live self-contained lives God does not exist
for them.[2]

Kierkegaard's purpose is to have existents see that their real interests can be met by faith in Christ. Only when existents view aesthetic existence as a "sickness unto death", as contrary to the possibility of authentic selfhood, can a response to the beneficial aspects of faith be made. However, Kierkegaard thinks that aesthetic existents must first realize that they need the remedy of faith. Cornelio Fabro, like Klemke, views Kierkegaard's notions of dread and despair in his psychological works as the key to the perplexing problems in the aesthetic works:

---

[1] E. D. Klemke, "Logicality vs. Alogicality, "Journal of Religion, Vol. XXXVIII, No. 1, (April, 1958), pp. 107-115.

[2] Ibid., p. 114.

A whole literature about Kierkegaard's thought, either superficial or insensible to the existential motives of his dialectic, could have been dispensed with if its authors had deigned to see this solution as the very argument of that masterpiece of theological phenomenology of sin, The Sickness Unto Death (1849). This admirable essay is the continuation, and in many respects the counterpart, of The Concept of Dread (1844), above all because it develops and determines the principle that "the opposite of sin is faith" and that the only remedy to the fatal madness of despair is the acceptance of faith. He, who, instead of withdrawing from sin by resorting to faith in his Saviour, rejects it, becomes the prey of despair (Fortvivlelse), which is for man the true sickness unto death.[1]

To the nominal Christian, the fact of the God-Man in history is an affront, not because he cannot understand it, but because he will not will to divert himself from aesthetic living:

> We may therefore conclude that the absurd of faith is for Kierkegaard an existential--
> that is, provisional or dialectical--irrational. It is such for a man who does not believe and because he does not believe.[2]

Kierkegaard sees the problem at hand as one of confronting aesthetic existents (who believe in a superfluous way but who do not have an authentic belief in Christ as the remedy of the despair intrinsic to their lives) with the fact that there is an existential paradox within which prevents them from seeing faith as an option which alone can cure their spiritual malady. Kierkegaard's religious works are evidence of this; an appreciation of them is crucial to an adequate understanding of Kierkegaard's aesthetic works and the implicit and unique argumentation involved therein.

---

[1] Cornelio Fabro, "Faith and Reason in Kierkegaard's Dialectic," A Kierkegaard Critique, ed. by Howard R. Johnson and Niels Thulstrup (New York: Harper and Brothers, Publishers, 1962), p. 189.

[2] Ibid., p. 185.

CHAPTER III

THE RELIGIOUS WORKS

In this chapter I will be dealing mainly with three of Kierkegaard's so-called religious works: Training in Christianity (1850), For Self-Examination (1851), and Christian Discourses (1848).[1] Evidence from these religious writings points to the fact that Kierkegaard posited faith as reasonable, and intended that this would only be implicit in his aesthetic works (hence, the difficulties in assessing his notion of faith correctly in the aesthetic works). Such evidence in the religious writings do afford us an opportunity to view the connection between Kierkegaard's primary purpose in writing pseudonymously and his notion of faith as reasonable.

Kierkegaard's precise notion of faith is one that refers not to unique, disparate acts that simply emanate from desperation and despair, but is one that consists of the maintenance of a way of life based on the reasonable decision to opt for that which is most advantageous, especially to one whom Kierkegaard had hoped to goad in his aesthetic works into recognizing clearly the exclusive alternatives that are only evident by acts of penetrating self-awareness. We shall also see that in the religious writings Kierkegaard conceives of faith as reasonable (not in a doctrinal sense, but in an existential one). In his aesthetic works he stressed the alogical character of faith to the point of having his pseudonymous authors speak of faith as "paradoxical," "absurd". This was a ploy to suade nominal Christians not really to consider faith as illogical or absurd, but to begin the work of penetrating self-awareness. In his psychological works, which

---

[1] Kierkegaard had intended that Concluding Unscientific Postscript (1846) would be his last work. Instead it turns out to be the turning point of his authorship. Two more pseudonymous works follow, i.e., Sickness Unto Death (1849) and Training in Christianity (1850), neither of which are aesthetic in nature. Other important religious works which follow are Purity of Heart is to Seek One Thing (1847), Works of Love (1947) and The Point of View for My Work As An Author (1848). These works, along with his Edifying Discourses (18 of them), which accompanied many of his works from 1843 to 1850, both pseudonymous and religious, constitute his religious works. These are markedly different not only in content but in methodology in that Kierkegaard writes directly concerning the truths of the Christian faith rather than attempting indirectly to elicit choices from his readers through his pseudonymous authors. [Walter Lowrie's A Short Life of Kierkegaard (New Jersey: Princeton Univ. Press, 1942, pp. 168 f.)]

are not aesthetic in nature but Kierkegaard's true thoughts, we see that Kierkegaard considers man as basically inauthentic. Christianity is paradoxical, but only in the sense that man <u>will</u> not alter his condition of false selfhood. The sacrifice and humility required to make the transformation from the state of sin to faith as its remedy is almost too much for aesthetic man, <u>especially</u> if Christianity is looked upon only as a body of doctrine. Kierkegaard must convince nominal Christians that Christianity is in its essence a matter of <u>willing</u> to turn from an inauthentic state to Christ as the Healer for that condition. Much of the confusion regarding Kierkegaard's emphasis upon passion and inwardness in his aesthetic works is a result of failure to assess correctly Kierkegaard's primary motive in these aesthetic works. Kierkegaard wishes to emphasize the limitations of reason in coming to understand the doctrines of faith. But this does not mean that Kierkegaard does not think that there is evidence for faith once man has recognized his inauthentic state. Reason, in spite of its limits, does point to the experience of inauthenticity and to the Christian message as relating to that malady as evidence of the fact that faith is a reasonable move. But nominal Christians are well aware of that Christian message. It is the lack of a true assessment of self which is lacking--thus the unique methodology in the aesthetic works. The religious writings evidence Kierkegaard's real intent throughout his writings--to have nominal Christians see, in the Christian message speaking to aesthetic man once man has begun to assess his individual condition of sin, the evidence for faith. Christianity is truly a dialogue between Christ as Healer and inauthentic man. Kierkegaard believes that once that confrontation is effected, faith will be viewed as reasonable. The religious writings, unlike the aesthetic works, are evidence of Kierkegaard's notion of the Christian message as essentially an existential one--it speaks directly to the spiritual crisis at the heart of man's being.

A. Kierkegaard's Primary Motive

In a comparison of Kierkegaard's religious and aesthetic works nothing is more apparent than that his real intent in his aesthetic works is not to give explicit reasons for the truth of Christianity but to prepare aesthetic existents for that decision which will be forthcoming once an honest assessment of self is rendered. In his journal writings,[1] Kierkegaard again and again emphasizes his singleminded purpose:

---

[1] Kierkegaard's journal writings were the record of his personal thoughts and some were ideas that he eventually hoped to incorporate in his published writings. Publication of them did not begin until after his death, and the work of publishing this voluminous journal output still persists today.

> The category of my work is: to make men aware
> of Christianity, and consequently I always say:
> I am not an example, otherwise all would be con-
> fusion. My task is to deceive people, in a true
> sense, into entering the sphere of religious
> obligation which they have done away with....[1]

Deception "in a true sense" refers to his singleminded motive of goading existents to <u>begin</u> authentic living by means of introspection, not to an abstruse motive in his work that leaves his readers in "confusion." And we can only truly understand Kierkegaard's positing of faith as reasonable when we recognize that his primary purpose in writing the aesthetic works is inextricably tied in with his notion of the Christianity of his day. Kierkegaard's charge is that modern Christianity had helped to delude man. Authentic Christianity exists only for the sick; only if man is made aware of his <u>need</u> for a cure can there be a rebirth of true Christianity. And aesthetic persons themselves have too well hidden the despair that is all around them to be discovered. As Kierkegaard says in a note in his journal:

> When one is actually sick and the sickness is
> serious, then one is very happy that there is
> a physician, but when one is not sick, has no
> idea at all of what it is to be sick--then
> "the physician" is really a disagreeable
> thought.[2]

Thus, consciousness of sin is the gateway to Christianity. For man, who is basically doubleminded in that he does not really seek the Good but in reality holds on to a false self that he pretends is authentic, only an existential moment of decisiveness can bring him the <u>possibility</u> of a needed cure.

Thus Christianity is relevant to an existent's life, but only after man has been made cognizant of his true condition. Christ is revealing himself as the <u>Truth</u>, and as the Truth which can only be known subjectively. When man once begins to see his helpless state, then, and only then, can Christ's healing power begin its work:

---

[1] <u>The Journals of Kierkegaard</u>, ed. by Alexander Dru, p. 175.

[2] <u>Kierkegaard's Journals and Papers</u>, Vol. I, A-E, ed. and trans. by Howard V. Hong and Edna H., Hong (Bloomington: Indiana University Press, 1957), p. 457.

> No, what is required is a predicament (<u>situation</u>): adventure upon a decisive action, so that thou dost become heterogeneous with the life of this world, unable any longer to have thy life in it, dost find thyself in conflict with it--then thou wilt be able to be observant of what I am here saying (says Christ). Perhaps also the tension will so affect thee that thou wilt understand that thou canst not support it without having recourse to Me, and so we can begin. Could one expect anything else of 'the Truth'?[1]

Kierkegaard's purpose is to make nominal Christians aware of the necessary condition for an authentic movement of faith. Kierkegaard feels that the choice of opting for faith or not cannot even be truly open to an individual who does not meet that condition:

> What Christ required as a condition for reaching the situation where there can be any question of becoming a Christian was a decisive action--there is now no longer any need of that.[2]

What decisive action? It is not the act of faith itself by which we become a Christian:

> What Christianity presupposes, namely the tortures of a contrite conscience, the need of grace, the deeply felt need, all these frightful inward conflicts and sufferings--what Christianity presupposes in order to introduce and apply grace, salvation, the hope of eternal blessedness--all this is not to be found, or is to be found only in burlesque abridgement--at bottom it is sheer superfluity which at the most one imagines the need of. And so in the end one becomes tired of Christianity; for the pressure of imitation was lacking, the idea, Christ as Pattern.[3]

---

[1] Kierkegaard, <u>For Self-Examination and Judge for Yourselves</u>, p. 200.

[2] Ibid., p. 203.

[3] Ibid., p. 209.

Kierkegaard is so insistent upon these <u>preliminaries</u> to an act of faith in his religious works, that it would be myopic for us not to see that these notions refer to his purpose in the aesthetic works. All Kierkegaard's efforts in denigrating reason and, as we shall see, in advancing the notion of subjectivity are done only with a view to have nominal Christians see Christianity in a new light and faith as a viable option for the spiritual malady that they now recognize:

> Not until man has become so utterly unhappy, or has grasped the woefulness of life so deeply that he is moved to say, and mean it: life for me has no value--not until then is he able to make a bid for Christianity.[1]

Kierkegaard's aim is to have nominal Christians see faith as an inescapable issue. As we have seen, the background for Kierkegaard's aesthetic works was the levels of existence and the interplay between them. In his religious works, in which he is speaking directly to Christian readers and exhorting them to the highest level of existence, he directly marks out why Christianity can be a panacea for the spiritual ills of aesthetic existence. And, whereas in his psychological works he had developed the notions of despair and dread so as to uncover the cause of man's spiritual illness, he now offers the potential remedy for them. Christianity offers to nominal Christians a cure for their despair and dread, but they must die first--die to themselves and the false image that they are holding up to themselves and the world. But the would-be authentic believer in Christ wants to hold on to the self that is of his own making. Thus Christ's healing is dialectical. His yoke is both easy and hard. It is hard because out of pride man wishes to cling to his false image. Thus, Christianity must first exhort man to die to that image. This is the necessary condition of an authentic belief in Christ Who alone can offer man a true self as related to Him. This is what Kierkegaard means when he says:

> For Christianity is not what we men, both thou and I, are only too prone to make of it, it is not a quack. A quack is at your service right away, and right away applies the remedy, and bungles everything.

---

[1] <u>Ibid</u>., pp. 120-121.

> Christianity waits before applying its
> remedy, it does not heal every wretched
> little ailment by means of eternity--
> this clearly is an impossibility as well
> as a self-contradiction--it heals by means
> of eternity and forever when the sickness
> is such that eternity can be applied--that
> is to say, to this end thou must first die.[1]

The aesthetic man knows all too well how to divert his attention from any possible cure of his spiritual malady. By engrossing himself in the immediate, he deadens the call to true spirituality and avoids the candid admission of the lack of true selfhood. In his religious work, <u>Judge for Yourselves,</u> Kierkegaard says:

> We have a suspicion of ourselves, we know
> fairly well within ourselves that we are
> not thoroughly sober. But then shrewdness
> and common sense and discretion come to our
> aid, so that by his help we can get something to hold on to--the finite. And then
> we walk straight and with confidence, without turning dizzy--we are entirely sober.
> But in case the absolute were absolutely to
> cast a glance at us (yet from this glance we
> withdraw, it is for this reason we hide among
> finite things, as Adam hid among the trees),
> or in case we were to cast a glance infinitely at the infinite (yet we keep ourselves
> from doing this, it is for this reason we
> busily employ our eyes upon errands in the
> service of finitude)--in case the absolute
> were to cast a glance at us or we at it, then
> it would be revealed that we are drunk.[2]

Kierkegaard views man as refusing to make the authentic spiritual move because of <u>willed</u> ignorance. It is more accurate to say that man is guilty <u>not just</u> because he is in the state of

---

[1] Ibid., pp. 99 - 100.

[2] Ibid., p. 129.

anxiety and despair, but also because he will not will to begin to seek a solution. The result of sin is again dialectical. It is the "sickness unto death," while at the same time there is an anguishing pleasure in the experience of a self that is no self at all:

> The deeper he then sinks in anxiety, the
> farther he removes himself from God and
> from the Christian position; he is most
> deeply sunken when he will not know any-
> thing higher, but on the contrary wills
> that this anxiety shall be, not merely
> the heaviest (which in truth it is not,
> for the heaviest is the pain of repent-
> ance), no, but that it shall be the highest.[1]

The anxiety which Kierkegaard talks of in Christian Discourses is the despair which Kierkegaard analyzes in Sickness Unto Death. It is essentially the longing to become nothing. The vain conceit of sin allows man to pursue the course which is all the time destroying him. But, even though man is heavy laden with despair, he is offended, in a respect, by the fact that he should alter his aesthetic condition. Kierkegaard depicts man in this condition as either refusing to become a self at all or else seeking a false self. At its base, this denial or falsehood of self is what constitutes self-love. Man is divorced from the Power which constitutes his being and refuses to seek a selfhood as related to that Power. Man is so heavily laden with sin that he needs a revelation concerning his condition; for sin is ignorance (although not in the Socratic sense). Sin, although man wills it freely, brings him under the thralldom of its power. The dialectic of sin consists in the fact that man experiences both the responsibility of his sinful acts and the necessity of submitting to its power. This confusion causes the lack of clarity regarding his inauthentic state. Christianity brings to the surface this condition with its revelation of sin; but man must first submit to a drastic change in his being before the spiritual malady can be cured:

> The natural man has also something he calls
> offence, something he calls love, etc.; but
> just as that which the natural man calls

---

[1] Søren Kierkegaard, Christian Discourses, trans. with an introduction and notes by Walter Lowrie (Princeton: Princeton University Press,]97]), p. 23.

> love is, Christianly understood, only self-
> love, so that which the natural man calls
> offence is no more than a temporary dispo-
> sition and only when Christ extols the rem-
> edy against this does the possibility of
> offence emerge; for it is in relation to
> this remedy that the decision must be made,
> whether to be a Christian or to be offended.[1]

This is just the condition Kierkegaard wished to have an aesthetic individual reach. And he wishes such a one to see for himself that there are two exclusive choices available--either continuing to be "offended" by what true Christianity offers, or else opting for a choice i.e., faith in Christ, which alone can alleviate the problem at hand. But, Kierkegaard had seen that the problem with reaching aesthetic existents was much more difficult then a direct accounting of Christ's life and resurrection could remedy, hence his decision to write pseudonymously in his aesthetic works. But, the aesthetic works along with the psychological works have the same purpose: Kierkegaard wants aesthetic existents to see that they must first come to terms with their individual spiritual condition. Then, and only then, can they view Christianity as a reasonable choice for that condition. Kierkegaard knows that Christ's life, death and resurrection are known sufficiently to the Christians of his day, but no amount of historical evidence, in this regard, can move the will. The fact that there might even be some evidence that weighs against Christianity is not of paramount importance. This is to look at Christianity as if it were primarily an object of scientific inquiry, which it is, but only secondarily. For Kierkegaard, Christianity is pleading with the sick heart of man, saying:

> Taste me and see--my cure is the perfect
> antidote for the illness which weighs you
> down. But you must believe! I will offer
> you evidence, but only the evidence of a
> cure which is consonant with your deepest
> spiritual needs. But that is evidence
> enough! First believe, and then you will
> see the rest!

But Kierkegaard views the will of an aesthetic individual as subtly avoiding the confrontation with the inescapable alternatives that would be present if an honest assessment of self were made:

---

[1] Kierkegaard, *Training in Christianity*, p. 113.

> For it is very far from being true that the
> longer a man deliberates and deliberates, the
> nearer he comes to God; on the contrary, the
> truth is that the longer the deliberations
> become while the choice is postponed, the
> farther he removes himself from God. To
> choose God is certainly the most decisive and
> the highest choice; but 'alas' for him who
> needs long deliberation, and 'woe' unto him
> the longer he needs it. For it is precisely
> faith's impatient quickness of judgement, the
> infinite sense of need which will hear of
> nothing else, that is not merely nearest to
> the choice but best prepared to choose.[1]

And irresolution leads to fickleness:

> For a long while it seemed perhaps as if irreso-
> luteness concealed in itself the elasticity of
> choice, or its possibility. That is now consumed,
> if ever it was there, the soul of the heathen
> is unstrung, it becomes evident what irresolute-
> ness really conceals in itself. In irresolute-
> ness there still is a power of holding out
> against thoughts, irresolution still makes an
> effort to be master in the house and to put
> thoughts in their place. But now masterlessness
> over the thoughts, or the whim of the moment,
> has assumed the government, whim rules--even
> with respect to the question whether to choose
> God.[2]

And then ensues the last step on this journey to spiritual degradation--disconsolateness. Paradoxically, Kierkegaard sees aesthetic existents as now wishing to maintain their false self in spite of inner torment. They wish only to forget what could have been their salvation:

> And then when fickleness has ruled long enough,
> and of course, like all ungodly rulers has
> sucked the blood and enfeebled the body,
> <u>disconsolateness</u> assumes the government. First

---

[1] Kierkegaard, <u>Christian Discourses</u>, p. 90.

[2] <u>Ibid</u>., p. 91.

> the heathen desired to be entirely rid of the
> thought of God; he desires now to sink down in
> the inanity of worldliness, there to seek for-
> getfulness, forgetfulness of the most dangerous
> thought, because it is the most uplifting of all
> thoughts, the thought of being remembered by God,
> the thought of existing before God.[1]

But Kierkegaard believes that man can see the Christian message as beneficial, but only once the work of self-examination has begun. His aesthetic works attest to his belief that although he considers Christianity essentially a dialogue between Christ and sinful man, nominal Christians cannot be communicated to by that message. The Christianity of his day, in his mind, has been sterilized. Kierkegaard's task is to replace the false image of essential Christianity as being doctrinal with an understanding of its essential content. Passion and subjectivity had to be stressed, in his mind, so that aesthetic persons could see Christianity in its true light and recognize the inner trappings by which inauthentic man avoids the healing grace of Christ. Kierkegaard believes that once man achieves this, the choice of faith as a possible remedy for the state of inauthenticity will be a meaningful one.

B. The Life of Faith

Kierkegaard sees faith in Christ as reasonable just <u>because</u> there is no overwhelming intellectual evidence <u>pro</u> or <u>contra</u>. Man's offense at the Christian message is not related to man's intellect being offended but to his spiritual reluctance to will a meaningful change. Christ forces man into an either-or situation. The cure is ever present (this is the <u>universal</u> aspect of Christ in that His cure is for all men at all <u>times</u>), but man can reject it. Kierkegaard sees the reasonableness of this confrontation. Man must be afforded the chance of deluding himself that it is <u>not</u> reasonable to choose Christ. An aesthetic individual can choose that avenue, but Kierkegaard does not feel that man is actually rejecting Christ on intellectual grounds. Kierkegaard clarifies his meaning of offense:

> But at the absolute the understanding stands
> still. The contradiction which arrests it is
> that a man is required to make the greatest
> possible sacrifice, to dedicate his whole life
> as a sacrifice--and wherefore? There is indeed
> no wherefore. 'Then it is madness', says the

---

[1]<u>Ibid</u>.

understanding. There is no wherefore, because there is an infinite wherefore. But whenever the understanding stands still in this wise, there is the possibility of offense. If now there is to be victorious advance, faith must be present, for faith is a new life.[1]

It is not the paradox of the union of God and man in one person that offends, but the demand of "the greatest possible sacrifice." The "wherefore" refers to the reasons that speculative thought would attempt to adduce in favor of the truth of Christianity. But no amount of evidence of this sort is appropriate when an aesthetic individual is confronted with a cure for his spiritual malady. Naturally the intellect will be offended at belief if it sets out to assess faith by using only objective criteria. Christ, as God-Man, is incomprehensible to the speculative mind; the union of the divine and human in one person cannot be understood by objective analysis. But, Christianity was never meant to be understood in this fashion:

> The God-Man is the sign of contradiction. And why? Because, replies the Scripture, He shall reveal the thoughts of hearts. Has, then, this modern notion about the speculative unity between God and man, all that about regarding Christianity merely as a doctrine--has it the remotest resemblance to the Christian?[2]

In this quote it is important that we carefully note Kierkegaard's establishing the connection of the "sign of contradiction" with the statement that "He shall reveal the thoughts of the hearts." The "sign of contradiction" assumes that man can *really* decide his spiritual destiny. Christ is the perfect Pattern to follow and believe in, only if man has the opportunity of rejection. And, it is commensurate with man's spiritual nature, his will, that Christ appeared in humility and lowliness. Christ made sure that He could not be merely admired. An externally regal revelation would not have rendered a genuine spiritual choice possible. The appeal of Christ is that He *did* come in the form of a servant. The fact

---

[1] Kierkegaard, *Training in Christianity*, p. 121.

[2] *Ibid.*, p. 126.

that he appeared in this manner is consonant with the choice that man must make in regard to his spiritual welfare. Miracles, the resurrection, etc., are part of the Christian revelation. But there is no evidence for or against them which has to do with the essential movement of faith. Man is still faced with a real decision as to whether to venture into the realm of faith. Kierkegaard feels if there is a cure for man's spiritual ills, there could be no more appropriate manifestation of it than in the Pattern of Christ:

> And so in one sense 'the Pattern' is behind more deeply downtrodden than ever any other man was, and in another sense before, infinitely exalted. But, 'the Pattern' must be behind in order to catch and encompass all. If there were one single man who truly could underbid or duck under by showing that in lowliness and humiliation he was still more humbly placed, then the pattern is no longer the Pattern, it is but an imperfect pattern, that is, a pattern only for a great multitude of men. Absolutely the Pattern must be behind in order to drive forward those who are to be fashioned in its likeness.[1]

"The Pattern must be behind" lest man's freedom be obviated. Kierkegaard's emphasis in <u>Concluding Unscientific Postscript</u> concerning the objective uncertainty of faith can be understood only in this context. Objective uncertainty in the most intense degree is most commensurate with the notion of despairing man who is yet still free to accept or reject salvation. Any degree of objective certainty concerning Christ as God-Man would be destructive to man's capacity to choose or reject freely. Christ's humiliation is essential. He cannot be <u>known</u>; He can only be <u>believed</u> in so that the possibility of <u>offense</u> remains intact. For Kierkegaard, then, the lowly aspect of Christ is the most reasonable aspect of His nature. We must be careful here that we do not misunderstand Kierkegaard's actual intent in glorifying Christ's lowliness and humility. He does not mean that nothing must be known concerning Christ. His words, His mission, are of paramount importance to the believer. Kierkegaard does not feel it is necessary in his aesthetic works to recount to Christians the beauty and structure of that life. Kierkegaard knows that nominal Christians feel an intellectual and emotional appeal in Christ. In a vague way they

---

[1] <u>Ibid.</u>, p. 233.

understand the spiritual needs He can fulfill. But the crucial aspect of faith is in the <u>willingness</u> to respond. All Kierkegaard's efforts are, in this regard, intended to awaken them from their spiritual slumber. The worth of the Physician is recognized by Kierkegaard and his audience; but Kierkegaard feels he knows the psychological trappings which prevent the patient from willing a real cure. It is man's will which will not respond.

Now, although Kierkegaard does emphasize the will vis-à-vis man's understanding of faith in a doctrinal way, his intention is to have the Christians of his day see faith as reasonable, as related to the choice of Christ as Healer for their inauthentic state. Reason is limited as far as an adequate understanding of the tenets of faith is concerned. To those who consider faith as a logical inquiry into doctrinal Christianity, Kierkegaard presents in his aesthetic works his antidote--stressing faith as paradoxical and absurd, so that nominal Christians might see it primarily as a <u>willed</u> response by inauthentic man to Christ the Healer--and as a reasonable response once a proper assessment of self has been effected. It is within this context that we must understand why Kierkegaard does not tire of relating in his religious works the resemblances of a Messiah who will not allow himself to be <u>understood</u> as God-Man:

> But now in the case of the God-Man! The true God cannot become directly recognizable; but direct recognizableness is what the merely human, what the men to whom He came, would pray and implore of Him as the greatest alleviation. And it was out of love He became man! He is love; and yet every instant He exists he must crucify as it were all human compassion and solicitude-- for He can only be the object of faith....But out there in the midst of that dreadful strife of decision He must hold men at a distance, if ever they are to belong to Him, as saved through faith--and He is love.[1]

In this manner, Christ <u>can</u> be a claim upon every man. Worldly or temporal loftiness of station would have negated any such claim. Thus, Christianity is immensely meaningful to

---

[1] Ibid., p. 137.

Kierkegaard because it perfectly suits man's condition, which is basically sinful. What kind of proof is this? Kierkegaard responds that when the Physician is present with a possible remedy, in this case an eternal remedy, one should not belabor the intellect with issues that are not commensurate with the crucial situation. Yes, it is reasonable to respond, according to Kierkegaard, but it is man's selfishness which is the obstacle. The "moment" is given to all to respond to. Man's sinful nature and Christ as the most perfect of Physicians make that moment decisive.

Man's choosing of faith, then, is not an irrational "leap", but one that is based on a choice of a life that can engender spiritual maturity and growth. Kierkegaard is clear in his religious writings that the life of faith is one that is marked by reasonably <u>willed</u> efforts to continue on the road to spiritual advancement. The real "leap" for Kierkegaard is the reversal from aesthetic living to the <u>beginning</u> of an honest assessment of self. A Christian's life, on the other hand, is a <u>becoming</u> marked by spiritual falls; but faith in Christ sustains him in the effort to live in the manner of Christ. The Christian lives at the highest level of existence because he alone knows how difficult it is to achieve perfect selfhood based on the Pattern of Christ's life. But this affords him an honest insight into what he really is. This explains why, for Kierkegaard, the Christian life is marked with suffering, while the aesthetic life is commensurate with adversity. The Christian truly realizes the brunt of his finiteness, and he has no delusions concerning his moral status; but along with this spiritual suffering is the assurance of forgiveness of sins. Kierkegaard's religious works are not an assertion of the sanctity of the Christian life, but a plea to allow Christ to work with individuals in their quest for authentic selfhood. Genuine faith is the willingness to allow Christ to aid in the struggle with sin, despair, and dread. And there is no doubt that in Kierkegaard's mind the act of faith is again and again a "test". There are no assurances or conclusive proofs, but there is the healing power of Christ that is offered to the despairing heart of man. And, in this context, faith is a step that follows once the dialogue of Christianity is truly operative. Once man's inauthenticity is perceived, he can listen meaningfully to Christ's essential message. Thus, the "leap" is not, in the manner of Pascal, the best bet from the vantage point that we have nothing to lose even if we are found wrong; for Kierkegaard, faith rewards those who seek deliverance from their inauthentic state. And the evidence of that inauthentic state, i.e., dread and despair, is not complicated for one who will begin an honest assessment of self. As Kierkegaard says, "Every time a man grasps this brief and pithy truth, that he can of himself do nothing, he understands himself."[1] This is why Kierkegaard finds the dictum of Christianity, "Thou shall believe", so commensurate with the existential needs of the existent burdened with sin and a heavy conscience. The function of Christianity, for Kierkegaard, is not to prove its claims, but to make that choice of faith an unavoidable one. Truly we can also say that the necessity for that choice is the very essence of Kierkegaard's purpose in writing.

In his religious works, then, the man of faith is no self-satisfied complacent existent, but one who best knows that faith demands courage and the ability to withstand the fear and trembling of the Christian life, the ever dangerous possibility of spiritual regression. But this should not make us think that, for Kierkegaard, the religious stage is alien to our "natural" life. This is why in all his eighteen edifying discourses,[2] which accompany the works throughout his authorship, there is constant reference to natural phenomen, e.g., the "birds of the air", "the lilies of the fields". Kierkegaard expands on religious themes by means of such natural phenomena. What is gained through faith is one's selfhood. This does not mean that reasoning, feeling and imagination are abrogated in order that the new life be lived. For Kierkegaard, the self is solidified by bringing all these functions together on the level of existence by means of choice.

From evidence gleaned from the religious writings we can see

---

[1] Søren Kierkegaard, Edifying Discourses, Vol. II, trans. by David F. Swenson and Julia Marion Swenson (Minnesota: Augsburg Publishing House, 1962), p. 151.

[2] Kierkegaard calls them "discourses" rather than sermons, because he does not use, in the majority of them, Christian dogmatic categories (although they obviously have a Christian intent), and they are not delivered by an ordained man. They are called "edifying" because they are spiritually uplifting only if the reader makes them so, whereas sermons have an intrinsic merit independent of the reader. The discourses' aim is to generate in existents the desire to raise the natural virtues of love, kindness, etc. to the religious level.

that, for Kierkegaard, the one work which man can do is to recognize his true spiritual state and will to act upon it. This is negative, but before the grace of faith can ensue, it must be. And there is evidence whether one has really performed this spiritual requirement or not. The grace of authentic faith is evidenced by patterning one's life after Christ. Kierkegaard feels imitation must be reintroduced, for the Christianity of his day has been infiltrated with a bogus notion of faith:

> Faith does not exist, what exists is at the most a mood which fluctuates between remembering Christianity as a thing already vanished, and expecting it as a thing to come. Imitation is an impossibility for when everything has been put in suspense, it is impossible for one to make a beginning with anything decisive, but one's existence drifts as it were with the current, and one employs one's natural self-love to make life as comfortable for one-self as possible.[1]

Imitation of Christ is a <u>manifestation</u> of the true spirit by which man humbles himself before the grace of faith. If one does not <u>live</u> Christianly, then genuine faith is absent. The grace of <u>faith</u> sustains an existent in his resolve to live after the Pattern of Christ. Kierkegaard is saying that it is not as if the imitation of Christ in daily life assures salvation, but it does <u>manifest</u> a genuine faith and is <u>evidence</u> of faith's humble <u>beginnings</u>. As Pattern, Christ is the One Whose life must be imitated as intensely as possible; but yet there is always the introspective movement by which the man of faith realizes that Christ is not just the model, but the Redeemer, whose saving grace gives man the opportunity to attempt the imitation, and without whose help his external works would be ineffective and ephemeral. In a journal entry in 1849, Kierkegaard mentions the "dialectical factor" of faith which has been disregarded by the Christian of his age--a candid spiritual introspection of self, which can engender genuine Christian belief, and faith itself are so interwoven that a notion of faith without recognizing this dialectical element can be indicative of inauthentic, aesthetic living:

---

[1] Kierkegaard, <u>For Self Examination and Judge For Yourselves</u>, pp. 204-205.

> The misfortune of Christianity is clearly that the dialectical factor has been taken from Luther's doctrine of faith so that it has become a hiding-place for sheer paganism and epicureanism; people forget entirely that Luther was urging the claims of faith against a fantastically exaggerated aesceticism.[1]

In summary, then, faith, for Kierkegaard, is not a whimsical act that has no reasonable preliminaries to it. It would be even more precise not to posit the locus of faith in a single act, although acts of faith are present again and again in man's striving for religious authenticity. Faith is a stance man takes toward himself and the world around him--a way of looking at existence. Just as the many individual acts of self-centeredness refer to the choice of a basically aesthetic existence, so do the acts of faith in Christ refer to the basic choice to seek the remedy for an impoverished spiritual condition. For Kierkegaard, these acts are manifestations of an influence that so dominates that it is the mirror through which a religious existent views himself and his world.

---

[1] The Journals of Kierkegaard, ed. by Alexander Dru, p. 166.

CHAPTER IV

SUBJECTIVITY

A reading of certain passages from Kierkegaard's aesthetic works would leave one with the impression that he meant his assertion of subjectivity as truth to be taken literally as the cornerstone of his epistemology. I believe we are now in the position, after having analyzed some of the aesthetic, psychological, and religious works, to assess that assertion within the light of the conclusions we have reached concerning Kierkegaard's motivation in his aesthetic works. I shall: (1) analyze Kierkegaard's view of subjectivity in <u>Concluding Unscientific Postscript</u> and argue that it is consonant with the purpose of his undertaking in the aesthetic work, in that it is intended to goad existents to begin the work of self-awareness so that the possibility of faith as a reasonable option can at least reveal itself; and I shall:(2) argue more specifically that Kierkegaard's notion of ethical subjectivity (in <u>Either-Or</u>, Volume II), especially in view of the inconsistencies in his aesthetic and non-aesthetic works, lends support to my thesis.

A. Subjectivity

It is not difficult to understand why Kierkegaard has been criticized as a radical subjectivist, one who holds that truth is proportionate to the intensity of one's passion and inwardness. Brand Blanshard views him in this light:

> He would remind us that religion is a commitment of the will, that "Christianity wishes to intensify passion to its highest pitch," not to induce in us belief or comprehension. But we have seen that this will not do. Christianity does include beliefs, and it insists rightly or wrongly that these beliefs are true in the common and ancient sense. To adopt Kierkegaard's new sense, peculiar to himself and inconsistently held, which reduces truth to a passionate commitment of feeling and will, would not save Christianity; on the contrary, it would largely destroy it. For it implies that there are no common truths for Christians to accept, no common principles by which their

lives may be guided, indeed no common Deity
for them to comtemplate and worship. The
Kierkegaardian subjectivity would dissolve
these things away into a set of processes in
individual minds where there would be as
many Christianities as there were persons to
exercise their "inwardness" and their passion.[1]

Blanshard's criticisms are all supported from passages in the aesthetic works, especially Concluding Unscientific Postscript. It is true that Kierkegaard, through Johannes Climacus, seems to be identifying truth with passion and inwardness. Kierkegaard says in the Postscript:

That subjectivity, inwardness, is the truth,
was my thesis. I have sought to show how the
pseudonymous authors, in my view, move in the
direction of this principle, which in its
maximum is Christianity. That it is possible
to exist with inwardness also outside Christianity
has among other things been sufficiently
demonstrated by the Greeks.[2]

Thus, the pseudonymous authors advocate passion for passion's sake. In the Postscript, Kierkegaard spells out no criteria by which to assess the value of Christianity over any other religious commitment:

If one who lives in the midst of Christendom
goes up to the house of God, the house of the
true God with the true conception of God in
his knowledge and prayer, but prays in a false
spirit; and one who lives in an idolotrous
community prays with the entire passion of the
infinite; although his eyes rest upon the
image of an idol; where is the most truth?

---

[1] Brand Blanshard, "Kierkegaard on Faith", p. 120.

[2] Kierkegaard, Concluding Unscientific Postscript, p.248.

> The one prays in truth to God though he
> worships an idol: the other prays falsely
> to the true God, and hence worships in fact
> an idol.[1]

And again in Either-Or, the same thesis is advanced in his discussion of choice:

> If you will understand me all right, I should
> like to say that in making a choice it is not
> so much a question of choosing the right as
> of the energy, the earnestness, the pathos
> with which one chooses. Thereby the persona-
> lity announces its inner infinity, and thereby,
> in turn, the personality is consolidated.
> Therefore, even if a man were to choose the
> wrong, he will nevertheless discover, precise-
> ly by reason of the energy with which he chose,
> that he had chosen the wrong.[2]

Yet in the Postscript he also seems to be distinguishing a type of passion that can lead to madness without spelling out any criteria by which one could assess authentic from inauthentic passion: "Don Quixote is the prototype for a subjective madness in which the passion of inwardness embraces a particular finite fixed idea."[3] And again in the same work he implies that faith must be related to truth in some confirmable way:

> ....for so much is certain, that if a little
> child (simply understood) is to provide the
> definition of what Christianity is, this
> will be without terror, for it will not con-
> tain that factor which was to the Jews a
> stumbling block and to the Greeks foolishness.[4]

---

[1] Ibid., pp. 179-180.

[2] Kierkegaard, Either-Or, Vol. II, p. 171.

[3] Kierkegaard, Concluding Unscientific Postscript, p. 175.

[4] Ibid., pp. 529-530.

What precisely is that factor? In his aesthetic works no answer is forthcoming. We do know that Kierkegaard feels that: "Christianity is still the only explanation of existence which holds water".[1] And, in another non-aesthetic work, he tells us that it is not passion for passion's sake he is advocating:

> The emotional seizure of the individual by something higher is far from defining a Christian adequately, for by emotion may be explained a pagan view, pagan conception of God. In order to express oneself Christianly there is required, besides the more universal language of the herd, also skill and schooling in the definition of Christian concepts, while at the same time it is of course assumed that the emotion is of a specific, qualitative sort, the Christian emotion.[2]

In these non-aesthetic works, Kierkegaard unequivocally spells out his denial of the identification of truth with subjectivity. In the same work he says:

> Christianity exists before any Christian exists, it must exist in order that one may become a Christian, it contains the determinant by which one may test whether one has become a Christian, it maintains its objective subsistence apart from all believers, while at the same time it is in the inwardness of the believer. In short, there is not identity between the subjective and the objective.[3]

---

[1] Søren Kierkegaard's Journals and Papers, Vol. I, p.457.

[2] Kierkegaard, On Authority and Revelation, p. 164.

[3] Ibid., p. 168.

Yet, the ambiguity exists in the aesthetic works, and because his assertions are so much more prominent than the few intimations he affords us in these works which could lead us to conclude that he is denying that identification, Blanshard's refutation of Kierkegaard is understandable. Nevertheless, we have seen in his non-aesthetic works that Kierkegaard's aim is to remedy the false Christianity he believed was infiltrating his time--a Christianity which was more involved with the speculative nature of beliefs themselves rather than with those beliefs bearing fruit in the lives of his individual countrymen. But, Kierkegaard is not denying the importance of those beliefs, nor is he setting out to destroy belief as Blanshard has argued. The emphasis on passion and inwardness is Kierkegaard's unique way of inducing Christians to <u>begin</u> an honest assessment of self so that there would be an opportunity to see the pressing need for an authentic faith in Christ. When Kierkegaard alludes to the "factor", he is referring to the awareness of the need for a remedy for a spiritless condition, but without explicating it. Kierkegaard intentionally had avoided discussion of the truths of the Lutheran faith not because he denied them, nor because he thought they had no relevance to the lives of his fellow Christians; his motive was to induce the Christians of his day to begin the introspective moment which would show the real relevance of those truths which had an appeal in a doctrinal way alone. This is the meaning of what Kierkegaard says in a religious work:

> It has constantly been maintained that reflection inevitably destroys Christianity and is its natural enemy. I hope, now, that with God's help it will be shown that a godfearing reflection can once again tie the knot at which a superficial reflection has been tugging for so long. The divine authority of the Bible and all that belongs to it has been done away with; it looks as though one had only to wait for the last state of reflection in order to have done with the whole thing. But behold, reflection performs the opposite service by once more bringing the springs of Christianity into play, and in such a way that it can stand up--against reflection. Christianity naturally remains completely unaltered, not one iota is changed. But the struggle is a different one; up to the present it has been between reflection and simple, immediate Christianity; now it will be between reflection and simplicity armed

with reflection.[1]

Kierkegaard had intentionally fought "reflection", i.e., Christianity merely as a body of truth to be studied, with "simple immediate Christianity", i.e., subjectivity, a more passionate awareness of self. Kierkegaard hopes that those truths which were held by nominal Christians could really be assimilated into individual lives. Subjectivity, in the real sense in which Kierkegaard uses that notion in the aesthetic works, is a necessary condition of truth, but not Christian truth itself. As a matter of fact, subjectivity alone leads to an awareness that one is not in the truth. In his analysis of despair and dread, Kierkegaard had brought us to the notion that a true examination of self leads to the awareness that one is inauthentic. But this is just where Kierkegaard intends to lead existents--to a recognition of the need for the Truth because of their impoverished spiritual condition. And, this is Kierkegaard's notion of what constitutes genuine subjectivity. Thus, Kierkegaard's aim in his explication of the notion of subjectivity throughout the aesthetic work is to bring aesthetic Christians to that point where they themselves could be aware of clear-cut alternatives once they did recognize their inauthentic state and could see the doctrines of faith in an entirely new light.

Henry Allison supports my critique of Blanshard's thesis by an analysis of Concluding Unscientific Postscript alone, without reference to Kierkegaard's psychological and religious works. Allison argues that Johannes Climacus's statement that "truth is subjectivity" leads to a "consistent misologism"--the identification of Christianity and nonsense. It is Allison's contention that the Postscript is the result of Kierkegaard's efforts at a reductio ad absurdum of theorizing in any way about Christianity. Allison agrees that Kierkegaard's purpose, as in all his aesthetic works, is to induce his readers to see what authentic Christianity essentially is in contrast to the Christianity taught and preached in a purely objective manner. There is no question in Allison's mind that Kierkegaard is emphasizing subjectivity to a point in the Postscript that one cannot distinguish it from nonsense:

> The first is again the oft mentioned problem
> of criteria. Climacus has so strongly
> emphasized the absurdity of the paradox that
> it would seem that any effort to distinguish
> its objective content from mere objective

---

[1] The Journals of Kierkegaard, ed. by Alexander Dru, p. 146.

considerations are irrelevant, and that it is
its subjective or existential significance
for the believer which distinguishes the
paradox from nonsense. This, however, gets
us nowhere, for it amounts to the admission
that <u>objectively</u> there are no criteria, and
hence the only difference between Christianity and nonsense is that the former happens
to be taken seriously by some individuals
while the latter is not.[1]

Although Kierkegaard, through Climacus, alludes to a distinction between Christianity and nonsense, Allison argues that the <u>Postscript</u> offers no criteria for judging in what sense Christianity is superior in light of Kierkegaard's emphasis upon subjectivity:

If belief really is an act of the will, which
by its very nature involves a "leap" beyond
the understanding, then far from inhibiting
belief, the recognition of the nonsensical
character of a doctrine would seem to provide
an inducement to inwardness and hence be a
potential source of "subjective truth." Thus,
we are led to the conclusion that not only
does Climacus' misologism distinguish between
the Christian absurd and nonsense, but that
even if such criteria were available, they
would be irrelevant to the subjective thinker.[2]

Allison is quite sure that Kierkegaard's intent is <u>not</u> to place Christianity in this light. His resolution of the problem is quite ingenious. It begins with an analysis of the name of the pseudonymous author of the <u>Concluding Unscientific Postscript</u>. Kierkegaard did not create the name "Johannes Climacus" <u>ex nihilo</u> but intentionally borrowed it from history. Johannes Climacus was a sixth century monk of the monastery at Sinai. The surname was derived from a title of a book

---

[1]
Henry Allison, "Christianity and Nonsense", <u>Review of Metaphysics</u>, Vol. XX., No. 3, Issue No. 79 (March, 1967), pp. 432-460.

[2]
<u>Ibid</u>., p. 453.

Scala Paradisi.[1] This suggests that Kierkegaard used the author's name in the Postscript to imply the approach to Christianity rather than its attainment. Climacus describes himself as a humorist (a non-Christian), one who has not himself made the leap to Christianity, although he is one who clearly sees the lack of relationship between the inward Christian life and its outward manifestations:

> Thus, the humorist knows something about the existential difficulties of the God-relationship. He is able to recognize objectivistic or superstitious perversions of this relationship, but he comprehends in an intellectual, i.e., objective, sort of way, what the believer appropriates existentially. Since the God-relationship lies in subjectivity, his very awareness of the difficulties of such a relationship requires a certain degree of inwardness, but since he does not himself make the "leap" but rather withdraws into the realm of jest, he is obviously lacking the decisiveness of the truly committed person. Now, given Climacus' own description of the stance of the humorist vis-à-vis Christianity, one would expect to find this reflected in his own analysis of faith, i.e., one would expect this analysis to be in its very essence humorous, and therefore, to some extent objective.[2]

The "objective" nature of Climacus' work is in its attempt to theorize about subjectivity. Christianity cannot be divorced from mere nonsense when such an attempt is made. It is impossible to communicate "existentially" the truths of Christianity in a meaningful way. To treat "subjectivity as truth", as a philosophical proposition, leads to the misologism that Allison sees in the Postscript:

---

[1] The English translation of this Latin title is Steps of Paradise.

[2] Henry Allison, "Christianity and Nonsense", p. 455.

> In proceeding in this way, however, it would seem that like the vast body of Kierkegaard's commentators, and "existential philosophers" in general, we have become "town criers of inwardness." We have attempted to treat as a philosophical proposition ("truth is subjectivity") what by its very nature cannot be regarded as such without contradiction. Is it any wonder then that <u>qua</u> philosophical proposition it reduces itself to an absurdity? The absurd consequences of this consistently misologistic position can now be seen to provide the repellent factor, the elusiveness necessary to indirection, which the author has artistically devised in order to avoid achieving a "result" and to throw his readers back upon themselves.[1]

Thus, according to Allison, Climacus' notion of the contradictory nature of Christianity is to be taken seriously. But it is a notion that Kierkegaard does not share, in that it is his purpose to show that conclusions reached (by a non-Christian) are the result of philosophizing. A conceptualization of Christianity in this way is impossible:

> Thus, unless we are to view Kierkegaard as guilty of the very stupidity which he went to such great lengths to condemn, we must view the whole "argument" as a jest, as an expression of the author's artistry, the intent of which is not to "prove" the superiority of Christianity or even to show us in a theoretical way that the absolute paradox makes a kind of sense as <u>supra rationem</u> which is lacking in garden variety nonsense, but rather to help us realize existentially what it means to become a Christian, and to see that the only valid concept which we can form about Christianity is that it defies conceptualization.[2]

---

[1] <u>Ibid</u>., pp. 458-459.

[2] <u>Ibid</u>., pp. 459-460.

Allison is correct when he argues that Kierkegaard's attempt is to show that authentic Christianity "defies conceptualization." When Christianity is looked upon as merely doctrinal, apart from its relationship to the individual who alone is cognizant of the experiences of dread and despair, then any attempt to describe it as the ultimate form of subjectivity fails. Of course, Kierkegaard does believe that Christianity is just that in that nothing is more passionate and subjective than the realization that one is in an inauthentic state and that one is confronted with a remedy for that spiritual malady. But, he realizes that the experiences of despair and dread cannot be treated "as a philosophical proposition." He believes that we can conceptualize in some manner about the inward life of an existent, but this is an attempt at alluding to experiences that Kierkegaard believes are common, yet ultimately private and incommunicable. Kierkegaard's intent is to point aesthetic existents in the direction where they do see faith as a reasonable venture, as a means out of a "predicament", which Kierkegaard feels can be beneficial if the will moves in the direction of faith. The confusion resulting from the issue of subjectivity can be avoided if we recognize that Kierkegaard is not presenting an epistemological theory; in actuality, his intention is to counter the image of the false Christianity of his day. Only then can nominal Christians recognize the reasonableness of a faith which addresses itself to individuals who experience the dread and despair (that Kierkegaard has alluded to in his psychological works).

B. Ethical Subjectivity

A dependence on Kierkegaard's aesthetic works alone is sufficient to warrant a derogatory judgment in regard to his ethical theory. His main ethical work, Either-Or, which is abstruse and vague in content, and Fear and Trembling, where Kierkegaard discusses "the teleological suspension of the ethical", lead Blanshard once again to speak of the tremendous limitations in Kierkegaard's works:

> The ethical level, says Kierkegaard, is the level of "the universal." By this cryptic pronouncement he seems to mean one or other of two things; either that the moral man will, in Kantian fashion, ask what conduct could in principle be consistently adopted by everybody, or, in Hegelian fashion, ask what the community would generally approve.

Most modern moralists would regard either
of these appeals as hopelessly inadequate,
but Kierkegaard had little grasp of ethical
theory. His chief contribution to it is to
say that at times it breaks down, and that
when it does, our resort must be a "teleological suspension of the ethical" at Divine
behest. The nature of this behest can be
ascertained only by faith.[1]

Is the criticism justified? Let us examine more closely
Kierkegaard's depiction of the ethical level of existence in
Either-Or.

Kierkegaard's portrayal of the ethical personality in
Either-Or is always vis-à-vis the aesthetic personality, the
young man against whom Judge William argues the ethical position.
For Kierkegaard, the aesthetic individual exercises his freedom
only upon objects that offer immediate satisfaction. In this
sense, he is determined. He is looking around him at all the
multifarious objects of satisfaction and is ready to choose only
those objects which deliver the optimum in momentary enjoyment.
The ethical person, on the other hand, has not all the alternative choices the aesthetic has because he is not primarily
interested in the moment. The only real choice for the ethical
individual is to choose himself as an authentic self which has
a nature not entirely fixed by temporal needs. An either-or
does not exist for the aesthetic individual because the only
genuine either-or is that choice which has as its object the
consolidation of the human personality in its essential nature.
Is the object of choice fulfilling to my nature as a spiritual
being or not? Now at the aesthetic level one's interests and
choices are all superfluous because such choices have no real
claim on one as an authentic existent. The aesthetic person is
not interested in searching for his eternal validity. Thus,
there are no real choices. There only remains the finite
temporal choices which never hit at the roots of the human
personality. Judge William, the advocate of the ethical life,
tells the aesthetic in Either-Or that:

> You have chosen....not to be sure, as you
> yourself will admit, the better part. But
> in reality you have not chosen at all, or
> it is in an improper sense of the word you
> have chosen. Your choice is an aesthetic
> choice, but an aesthetic choice is no choice.
> The act of choosing is essentially a proper
> and stringent expression of the ethical.

---

[1] Brand Blanshard, "Kierkegaard on Faith", pp. 114-115.

> Whenever in a stricter sense there is question of an either/or one can always be sure that the ethical is involved.[1]

The aesthetic person is not necessarily the purely sensuous but anyone who refuses to withdraw into himself and attempts to find the essential meaning of existence. He could be poet, businessman or philosopher. The point is that such a personality should not even be called "individual" because he has not attempted to discover his authentic selfhood. Not only is such a personality devoid of real authentic individuality, but he is at heart a deceiver. This is what Kierkegaard means when he says:

> But above all, for your own sake, for the sake of your salvation--for I am acquainted with no condition of soul which can better be described as perdition--stop this wild flight, this passion of annihilation which rages in you: for this is what you desire, you would annihilate everything, you would satiate the hunger of doubt at the expense of existence.[2]

The "hunger of doubt" refers to the attitude of the aesthetic to direct his will only to those objects which offer immediate fulfillment. The "passion of annihilation" is the condition of never finding rest in any of the temporal joys of life, for there might always be something better around the corner. The aesthetic "annihilates" because all choices end up in boredom. The moment a choice is made, the object of that choice becomes as nothing. The real "annihilation" that Kierkegaard is concerned with is annihilation of the spirit. The aesthetic is a man without spirit because he refuses to live on that level which engenders true spiritual life. The aesthetic personality is on a pinnacle, as it were, surveying the various objects of choice that parade before him. Yet none of them yields an authentic choice. This is so because a spiritual being cannot rest permanently in any temporary fulfillment. The aesthetic has the mind and heart of a dilettante. Transitory objects are his excuse not to look within where true ethical subjectivity lies.

---

[1] Søren Kierkegaard, <u>Either-Or</u>, Vol. II, p. 170.

[2] <u>Ibid.</u>, p. 164.

What is the temptation which is present which could entice one to live on this level rather than on the ethical? Uniqueness. The aesthetic personality lives not by duty but by those factors which augment his singular importance. The ethical personality is not impressed with this. He is primarily interested in performing universal duty, combining the temporal (the finite self with all its limitations and talents) with the eternal. In a real sense there is no uniqueness to this at all and Kierkegaard, through Judge William, recognizes this:

> Yes, verily, it requires much ethical courage to acknowledge the good as the highest, because thereby one falls under perfectly general catagories. To that people stoutly object, they would like to have for themselves the distinction of difference for everyone can be a good man who wills it, but it always requires talent to be bad. Hence, many would like to be philosophers, not Christians, for to be a philosopher talent is required, to be a Christian humility, and that everyone can have who wills it.[1]

The ethical personality is not primarily interested in the cultivation of the unique talents which he is afforded, but in the admission of their relative unimportance. What is important is to choose in an authentic manner. And really choosing is choosing oneself as an individual. But the genuine individual finds himself only through the universal. He truly discovers himself when in an unobtrusive manner he performs universal duty. Thereby he does not lose his concreteness, nor is his authentic individuality in any sense lost. The reverse is true:

> He who regards life ethically sees the universal, and he who lives ethically expresses the universal in his life, he makes himself the universal man, not by divesting himself of his concretion, for then he becomes nothing, but by clothing himself with it and permeating it with the universal. For the universal man is not

---

[1] Ibid., p. 231-232.

> a phantom, but every man as such is the
> universal man, that is to say, to every
> man the way is assigned by which he be-
> comes the universal man. He who lives
> aesthetically is the accidental man; he
> believes himself to be the perfect man
> by reason of the fact that he is the only
> man. He who lives ethically labors to
> become the universal man.[1]

It would seem that Kierkegaard is assuming that man's consciousness is such that it can find repose by doing duty. He never outlines for us many of the duties because he assumes that man can discover them. In Either-Or Judge William is primarily interested in the duty of loyalty as it exists in the married state. This is the point of departure for the Judge to expatiate on duty in general. Man can comprehend universal duty if he wills to live authentically. The ethical personality knows that spiritual living entails genuine sacrifice and living for others as well as self. What keeps the aesthetic man from this recognition is pride--pride in one's own unique ability and the dubious satisfaction that comes from viewing life in a cynical, haughty manner. The essential trait of the ethical personality is humility, the willingness not only to recognize the truth in its universal form, but to actually will to do that which effects a certain indifference to any unique talents that might be evident, but which are for the ethical personality still part of the temporal flux, and hence relatively unimportant.

The essential and most adequate expression for the aesthetic personality is "mood". Because the aesthetic personality is affected by only the transitory, it alone can absorb him. Thus, he is lost always in the moment. It must always be taken with infinite seriousness, for there is nothing else, and man's spirit must be sublimated in some fashion. What is left except losing oneself as best one can in all the circumstances of one's temporal life? This is what Kierkegaard means by mood. But of course man being spirit, this is ultimately unsatisfying, although initially tempting. It is not that the ethical personality is not influenced by mood. He is. But he puts it into proper perspective. It has only a relative importance for him,

---

[1] Ibid., p. 260.

not an absolute one. Still, there is continuity between levels of existence for Kierkegaard in this aesthetic work. The aesthetic life is not lost but discovered for what it is by the ethical personality:

> For he who lives aesthetically seeks as far as possible to be absorbed in mood, he seeks to hide himself entirely in it, so that there remains nothing in him which cannot be inflected into it....He too, who lives ethically experiences mood, but for him this is not the highest experience; because he has infinitely chosen himself he sees the mood below him....He who lives ethically does not annihilate mood: he takes it for an instant into consideration, but this instant saves him from living in the moment, this instant gives him mastery over the lust for pleasure, for the art of mastering lust consists not so much in annihilating it, or entirely renouncing it, as in determining the instant.[1]

We can see now more clearly why Kierkegaard claims the aesthetic personality is both choosing and not choosing. When the aesthetic chooses he is choosing only in a wide sense of that term. He can do what he wishes, but there are no authentic alternatives involved in his choices. He must choose the superficial and inconsequential because he is a person who has willed to live on the aesthetic level. His moral stature in life is to live for the moment and to be aesthetic. To reach genuine, ethical subjectivity, he must not so much alter his particular choices, but his entire outlook upon life. Aesthetic choices are those without passion and energy because such traits are present only when one seeks essential identity. This is what Kierkegaard means when he says:

> What is it, then, that I distinguish in my either/or? Is it good and evil? No, I would only bring you up to the point where the choice between the evil and the good acquires significance for you. Everything hinges upon this. As soon as you can get

---

[1] Ibid., p. 234.

a man to stand at the crossways in such a
position that there is no recourse but to
choose, he will choose the right.[1]

Good and evil are posited only when one takes an ethical
stance. And one takes an ethical stance when one's acts are
directed to fulfilling one's nature. By "good" and "evil"
Kierkegaard means particular acts. The aesthetic, because his
interest does not reside in the fulfillment of his identity,
does not even distinguish between a good act and a bad one. His
interest lies elsewhere. It would be more apt to term the
aesthetic personality "amoral" rather than immoral. Only an
ethical man can make this distinction, for he is attempting to
direct his energy toward duty and the fulfillment of self. He
can commit evil because his will might fail in its attempt to
satisfy the moral law. The aesthetic does not commit evil acts
in this sense. Rather, he resides in amorality because he fails
to focus his will in the only direction where good and authentic
fulfillment have meaning. Kierkegaard says:

> It is, therefore, not so much a question of
> choosing between willing the good or the
> evil, as of choosing to will, but by this
> in turn the good and the evil are posited.
> He who chooses the ethical chooses the
> good, but here the good is entirely abstract
> only its being is posited, and hence it
> does not follow by any means that the
> chooser in turn cannot choose the evil, in
> spite of the fact that he chose the good.
> Here you see again how important it is
> that a choice be made, and that the crucial
> thing is not deliberation but the baptism
> of the will which lifts up the choice into
> the ethical.[2]

What is the ethical choice for Judge William? The only true
passion associated with the will is the passion of choosing
oneself:

---

[1] Ibid., p. 172.

[2] Ibid., p. 173.

> The energy with which I became ethically
> conscious is, therefore, the thing that
> counts, or rather, I cannot become
> ethically conscious without energy. I
> can, therefore, never become conscious
> of my eternal nature.[1]

Passion and inwardness mean, then, being passionate and inward the <u>right</u> way. The aesthetic cannot be authentically passionate because he is essentially under the category of necessity. Only the ethical man is authentic because he is truly existential and lives under the category of freedom. Only the ethical personality realizes the struggle of the moral life because he alone attempts to be moral. And he realizes the difficulty, time and time again, in the moral life. His passion and energy must be utilized again and again in order for him to abide by moral law. This is what Kierkegaard means when he states that, "He, therefore, who has chosen himself is <u>eo ipso</u> active."[2]

There are three important conclusions to be derived from an analysis of Kierkegaard's treatment of the ethical personality: (1) Kierkegaard is vague as to the specific quality of acts that are ethical, and, apart from his rather general description of the universal man satisfying his eternal validity, he offers no criteria as evidence of a good or bad act; (2) His emphasis is again and again upon the necessity of choosing--even to the point of his assertion that if one really chooses, he will choose correctly; and (3) These themes are set against the aesthetic personality who has not chosen at all. But can we not defend these elements in his ethical work as consonant with the major thrust of his teaching? Kierkegaard's depiction of the universal man is intentionally vague because he is not interested in presenting an ethical theory. As I have said, he wishes to provoke aesthetic existents so that they might <u>begin</u> to discover introspectively that they lack authenticity. That is why he so loosely asserts that when one chooses with passion he chooses rightly. He is primarily interested in aesthetic

---

[1] <u>Ibid</u>., p. 274.

[2] <u>Ibid</u>., p. 236.

existents and their lack of an authentic Christian existence as evidenced by a passionate struggle to sustain themselves against the ever-present dangers of spiritual shallowness, i.e., their very aestheticism. Thus, he is intent on spurring them on so that his plea for individual ethical effort will be transformed into the beginning of religious subjectivity--the awareness of their inauthenticity.

But there is another evidence of Kierkegaard's intent in this regard and that consists in the inconsistencies which appear when he explicates his notion of despair in <u>Either-Or</u>. As we saw in his psychological works, despair is at the level of aesthetic existence vis-à-vis the Christian level of existence. Kierkegaard seemingly contradicts this identity between despair and aesthetic living when he says in <u>Either-Or</u>:

> Behold, my young friend, this life of yours is despair. Hide this if you will from others, from yourself you cannot hide it, it is despair. And yet in another sense this life is not despair. You are too frivolous to despair, and you are too melancholy not to come in touch with despair.[1]

Here he contrasts melancholy, which is despair in a pejorative sense, with the despair that leads man to ethical living. Melancholy is the result of the rejection by an aesthetic personality of heeding the demand of the spirit to live ethically and non-aesthetically:

> What then, is melancholy? It is hysteria of the spirit. There comes a moment in a man's life when his immediacy is, as it were, ripened and spirit demands a higher form in which it will apprehend itself as spirit. Man, so long as he is immediate spirit, coheres with the whole earthly life, and now the spirit would collect itself, as it were, out of this dispersion and become in itself transformed, the personality could

---

[1] <u>Ibid</u>., pp. 209-210.

be conscious of itself in its eternal validity.[1]

Those who consciously recognize the despair of aesthetic living for what it is, inauthentic existence, have the opportunity to elevate themselves to the beginning of the ethical life. Too often, however, the movement is checked. The humility required and the lack of uniqueness that is essential to a life of duty, curtails any movement to the ethical level. Kierkegaard, through Judge William, sees the overt emotion of melancholy abating, but the deeper ontological dissatisfaction with self remains:

> This joy you have now chosen, this laughter of despair. You return again to life, under this illumination existence acquired a new interest for you. Just as you find great joy in talking to a child in such a way that what you say is understood by it very well and easily and naturally, while for you it means something entirely different, so you find joy in deceiving men by your laughter.[2]

But yet, Kierkegaard speaks of despair that is consistent with ethical living. It is the despair of the finite, the temporal in man. The ethical existent must continuously overcome the hindrance that every man feels who attempts to live ethically, to choose himself as an authentic self. Despair of this sort is authentic. Only those who despair over the essential finitude of their being and yet continue to attempt to make ethical choices (although not always successful) have succeeded in ascending to the ethical level of existence.

> So, then I bid you despair, and never more will your frivolity cause you to wander like an unquiet spirit, like a ghost, amid the ruins of a world which to you is lost. Despair, and never more will your spirit sigh in melancholy, for again the world will become beautiful to you and joyful, although you see it with different eyes than before, and your liberated spirit will soar up into the world of freedom.[3]

---

[1] Ibid., p. 193.

[2] Ibid., p. 223.

[3] Ibid., p. 223.

Melancholy, or despair in an aesthetic sense, will never envelope the ethical personality, because he is making an effort to posit his spirit in an authentic way, to despair over the finite and the temporal within himself.

But Kierkegaard's depiction of despair in <u>Sickness Unto Death</u> is quite different. As we have seen, despair as analyzed by Kierkegaard in this work is the result of continously refusing to will in harmony with God. To will in the authentic modes delineated by Kierkegaard in <u>Sickness Unto Death</u> is the act of a self which refuses to take cognizance of its essential nature, i.e., both soul and body united by spirit. Never to bother about living religiously is to live in aesthetic despair. The true either-or in this psychological work excludes the ethical and the despair involved thereunto in <u>Either-Or</u>.

Kierkegaard's treatment of the boundaries between the levels of existence in <u>Concluding Unscientific Postscripts</u> points out another inconsistency. Irony and humor[1] are both attitudes of the spirit which mirror an individual's response to the incongruity of authentic living and finitude. Between the aesthetic and ethical level is irony; between the ethical and religious level, humor. In regard to irony Kierkegaard says:

> For the ethicist does indeed reveal himself in so far as he pours himself forth in the tasks of the factual reality in which he lives; but this is something that the immediate individual also does, and what makes him an ethicist is the movement of the spirit, by which he sets his outward life inwardly in juxtaposition with the infinite requirement of the ethical, and this is

---

[1] As is the case with the presentation of the levels of existence in the aesthetic works, Kierkegaard's depiction of irony and humor is not to be taken as his own view. As we shall see, the inconsistencies to be noted are those of Johannes Climacus, not Kierkegaard. That Kierkegaard could be so flagrantly inconsistent in regard to the notions of despair and the boundaries between the levels can be adequately explained only if we again recognize that Kierkegaard is "using" the pseudonymous authors for his unique purpose.

something that is not directly apparent.¹

Both the aesthetic and the ethical personalities recognize the ironic situation of the juxtaposition of the finite along with the infinite ethical requirements set upon man. Even though this is a kind of despair, the ethical existent refuses to give in to the more immediate solution of disregarding entirely the attempt to live authentically. Despite the arduousness of the task, the ethical existent sets his sights on self-fulfillment. The aesthetic, on the other hand, has no desire for discovering his true self. The irony of the situation is too much. The demand to fulfill inwardly the ethical requirement without any external sign or evidence leaves aesthetic individuals cold. They would rather be something when they are being observed. But the only true ironist is the ethical existent who delicately maintains the balance between finite living and subjective, ethical living. As in Either-Or, such a person discovers true selfhood through the fulfillment of ethical duties.

When Kierkegaard begins to explicate this notion of humor,² some interesting results appear. Humor is the spiritual attitude of realizing that the task of continuously performing ethical duty is too difficult. It is the juxtaposing of the actual duty required day in and day out against the manner in which the self continuously misses the mark. A humorist will either maintain this attitude at the ethical level, or use humor as a stepping stone to the Christian level of existence:

> When humor uses the Christian terminology
> (sin, the forgiveness of sin, atonement,
> God in time, etc.), it is not Christianity

---

¹Kierkegaard, Concluding Unscientific Postscript, p. 450.

²Kierkegaard, through Johannes Climacus, uses the term to note the attitude of those who recognize the essential connection between existence and suffering; but rather than comprehending suffering as a result of the inevitable plight of those related both to the eternal and temporal (and hence its religious significance), the humorist attempts to revoke the reality of suffering in the form of jest. (Kierkegaard, Concluding Unscientific Postscript, pp. 400-402, 448, 451, 454).

but a pagan speculation which has acquired a knowledge of the Christian ideas. It can come deceptively close to the Christian position; but where decisiveness takes hold; where existence, while the bridge of immanence and recollection is burned behind him; where the decision comes to be in the moment, and the movement is forward toward a relationship with the eternal truth which came into being in time: there humor does not follow.[1]

It would seem that by using the phrase "bridge of immanence and recollection" Kierkegaard is referring both to the ethical personality <u>and</u> to those who have entered the level of Religiousness A. In either case, despair sets in--at the ethical level because of the difficulty of his task, at the level of Religiousness A because he does not find God immanently. Kierkegaard is now telling us, in contrast to his view of the ethical life in connection with his notion of irony, that the ethical life, with its rigid demands and our inability to follow them in an adequate manner, can never become a satisfying existence. The ethical life, though a level beyond the aesthetic, is also inadequate in the long run. But, of course, Kierkegaard is not precise because he did not feel the need to be when he was neither presenting a theory of the ethical level (nor one of the level of Religiousness A). The important point is that Kierkegaard's exposition of the ethical level is not to be interpreted as a theory of ethics. His depiction of the ethical life is to motivate nominal Christians to a life of inwardness wherein the discovery of sin and despair might be effected. The same holds true in regard to that level beyond the ethical, Religiousness A. When Cornelio Fabro sums up Kierkegaard's thoughts on the relationship between faith and reason, he takes literally Kierkegaard's exposition of the level of Religiousness A:

> For Kierkegaard, Religiousness A is true religiousness, and in the spiritual substance of man it has the same positive value that it had in the course of history. Still better: it has a propaedeutic value, which Kierkegaard considers indispensable in relation to Religiousness B. He gives the importance of a principle

---

[1] Kierkegaard, <u>Concluding Unscientific Postscript</u>, p. 243.

> to this propaedeutic: in order to have authentic Christians capable of taking upon themselves the responsibilities of Christianity, it is first of all necessary to have authentic men ready to fulfill the duties that come from human nature as such. Religiousness A must already be present, therefore, before any attention can be given to the dialectic of the other. It is necessary that the individual be already in relation with the eternal beatitude in the purest expression of an existential <u>pathos</u>, as was the case with Socrates before any questions can arise of this dialectic raised to the second power (Christianity) which throws a man into the <u>pathos</u> of the paradox. Many Christians make the mistake of wanting to become Christians all at once, without passing to Christianity by way of Religiousness A, and without satisfying its exigencies.[1]

But in Kierkegaard's religious works there is no discussion of this level as an avenue through which one must travel to attain the Christian level of existence. The ethical level and the level of Religiousness A are not stages through which aesthetic existents must ascend before attaining the level of Religiousness B, Christianity. His analysis of those levels is for the purpose of directing aesthetic existents to begin that which is a necessary condition of authentic Christian faith, i.e., penetrating introspection. The pseudonymous authors alone (not Kierkegaard) advance cases for the two levels beyond the aesthetic. But, for Kierkegaard, there are only two levels, the aesthetic and the Christian. His purpose, through the pseudonymous authorship, is to have aesthetic existents become passionate, strive for self-fulfillment, so that the need for Christ as a remedy for sin be manifested. Christ's commands of love and faith alone are the answer to an aesthetic individual's spiritual crisis. As we saw in Kierkegaard's religious works, such commands are directed to a being who is imbedded in sin and despair, and whose relationship to the eternal is tenuous. In his religious work, <u>Works of Love</u>, Kierkegaard posits the exact

---

[1] Cornelio Fabro, "Faith and Reason in Kierkegaard's Dialectic", p. 191.

relationship he feels exists between despair, man's need for salvation, and Christian duty:

> Despair is, namely, not something which may happen to a man, an event like fortune and misfortune. Despair is a disproportion in his inmost being--so far down, so deep, that neither fate or events can encroach upon it, but can only reveal the fact that the disproportion--was there. Therefore, there is only one assurance against despair: to undergo the change of eternity by the "shalt" of duty;....despair consists in not having undergone the change of eternity by duty's "shalt." Consequently despair is not the loss of the beloved, this is misfortune, pain,suffering; but despair is the lack of the eternal.[1]

Duty's "shalt" refers primarily to the commands of following Christ's life and love. We must be commanded to love (and Kierkegaard thinks that nominal Christians can feel the appropriateness of such a command once they recognize that they are not capable of fulfilling the law of love). Kierkegaard's desire in his religious works is basically to show us how in every possible way the life of Christ meets the demands of the spiritual life. Even though Kierkegaard continuously uses the term "God" throughout his aesthetic works, it is not a given, nor the result of any theoretical argument (for Kierkegaard abhors any attempt to reach God this way). Aesthetic individuals can reach God only subjectively, by the passionate discovery of their inauthentic state and the resultant choosing of Christ as the balm for their spiritual distress.

Concluding Unscientific Postscript and Either-Or both are to be regarded as approaches to the Christian position that Kierkegaard finally reached in his religious works. They are attempts at inducing Christians to begin Christian living by examining their inauthentic state. While in the earlier work, Either-Or, the emphasis is upon ethical subjectivity, in the Postscript, the emphasis is upon the relationship between subjectivity and Christian living. But the intent in both is the same. The Postscript, the last of his aesthetic works, comes

---

[1] Søren Kierkegaard, Works of Love, trans. by David F. Swenson and Lillian Marion Swenson, (Princeton: Princeton University Press, 1949), p. 34.

closer to Kierkegaard's actual position. But the conclusions we can draw from it are not Kierkegaard's own view. Climacus' emphasis is upon the need for living at the height of individual passion and inwardness and Christianity's answer to that need:

> The task of becoming subjective, then, may be presumed to be the highest task, and one that is proposed to every human being; just as, correspondingly, the highest reward, an eternal happiness, exists only for those who are subjective; or rather, comes into being for the individual who becomes subjective.[1]

But, for Kierkegaard, the highest degree of passionate living, i.e. being passionately concerned about one's eternal destiny, is not commendable, as would seem in the Postscript, for its own sake. But Kierkegaard believes that if aesthetic existents begin to be concerned passionately about themselves and their eternal destiny, the tremendous need for Christ as the remedy for despair and dread will become evident, i.e. true subjectivity. In Either-Or, Kierkegaard's purpose is the same. If aesthetic existents attempt ethical living, the failure in living up to ethical demands by one's own unaided efforts can effect a religious response to Christ's healing power. Even in the Postscript, where Kierkegaard speaks of Either-Or as if he were in no way responsible for its production, he tells us that ethical subjectivity is only beneficial in that it can direct existents to a life of faith:

> Had Either-Or proposed to make it clear where the difficulty lies, the entire work would have had to have a religious orientation; but in that case it would have been necessary to say in the beginning what, according to my ideas, should be said only successively. The difficulty was now not at all touched upon, and this was quite in accordance with my own plan. Whether this has been clear to the author, of course I cannot tell. The difficulty is, that the ethical self is supposed to be found immanently in the despair, so that the

---

[1] Kierkegaard, Concluding Unscientific Postscript, p. 146.

>individual by persisting in his despair at least wins himself....But this avails nothing. When I despair, I use myself to despair, and therefore I can indeed by myself despair of everything; but when I do this, I cannot by myself come back. In this moment of decision it is that the individual needs divine assistance.[1]

Kierkegaard's notion of subjectivity presents a problem only if we regard Kierkegaard as presenting a theory of truth, religious or otherwise. Both Climacus and Judge William are non-Christians who do not fully appreciate the notion of faith. And this is Allison's point. Any attempt by non-Christians to theorize about the relationship between subjectivity and Christianity is bound to fail without a precise notion of the categories of despair and dread. Climacus' exposition on subjectivity is incomplete without an individual experience of sin which points out the need for the healing grace of Christ.

To see Kierkegaard as identifying subjectivity, i.e. passion and inwardness, with truth is the result of myopically viewing the Postscript as Kierkegaard's own position. The inconsistencies I have noted in this chapter lead us to the conclusion that Kierkegaard sees concern for one's ethical and religious stature as a preliminary to faith in Christ. "Subjectivity is truth" is not an epistemological position advocating passion for passion's sake; rather it is an implicit plea to individuals to commence the work of Christian rebirth so that faith can be viewed primarily as that which can best satisfy their deepest spiritual yearnings.

---

[1] Ibid., p. 230.

CHAPTER V

FAITH AND REASON

In this chapter I shall: (1) assess the meaning of reason in relation to faith by an evaluation of a philosophical work by Herbert Garelick which relates to many of the problems I have suggested in regard to that notion; (2) examine more closely the options present before the act of faith ensues--entries from Kierkegaard's Journals will serve as evidence that Kierkegaard was attempting to elicit from nominal Christians the choice of faith based on the reasonable nature of that response; and, (3) explicate Kierkegaard's implicit argument for faith, concluding with a brief assessment of it and a few summary comments.

A. Reason in Kierkegaard

Herbert Garelick's argument is an attempt to show that Kierkegaard's Concluding Unscientific Postscript is an affirmation of the value and use of reason in regard to faith. It is Kierkegaard's use of subjectivity in the Postscript which leads Garelick to the conclusions he reaches. Summing up the notion of subjectivity in the Postscript, Garelick says:

> Subjectivity is a passionate concern for one's being. One is subjective if and only if his death and his desire for eternal happiness is of sole concern. At every moment of living in whatever he is doing a subjective individual is absolutely interested in his eternal happiness... The subjective individual cannot absolutely be interested in both his eternal happiness, "absolute telos", and various relative ends. To be interested in relative ends even part of the time is to be only partly interested in the absolute end, thereby, degrading that end into a relative end....[1]

---

[1] Herbert M. Garelick, Anti-Christianity of Kierkegaard, (The Hague: Martinus Nijhoff, 1965), pp. 19-20.

Kierkegaard, through Johannes Climacus, states that subjectivity comes to the fore to meet the problems of existence. Since man's mortality is, as Garelick says, "the problem of existence which is insoluble by speculative reason,"[1] subjectivity alone is equipped to handle this difficulty. Now man's passionate yearning for eternal happiness encounters Christianity which offers faith in the Paradox of the God-man in history. But to accept the Paradox is, at least in the Postscript, to sacrifice our intellect. As Climacus says in the Postscript: "But Christianity also requires that the individual risk his thought, venturing to believe against the understanding."[2] Garelick argues that, in the Postscript, Climacus views reason as able to make judgements not about the existence of the Paradox, but only about its rationality. By this, Garelick means that using reason alone as a criterion, one can view the paradox as irrational but not, therefore, impossible. Irrationality refers to logical impossibility, not existential impossibility. Garelick cites various assertions by Kierkegaard in the Postscript in which reason is limited merely to logic. But, God's existence and reality are beyond the canons of logic. Given the fact that the paradox is not an impossibility but only irrational, Garelick argues that Kierkegaard's emphasis upon subjectivity is a device to show that Christianity is, in reality, a reasonable enterprise:

> Since abstract reason does not answer our concern, perhaps non-reasonable claims do; and perhaps they do. Since reason must be restricted to the speculative realm and not extended to existence, the decision to embrace its opposite is a rational movement dictated by our desire to discover eternal happiness. As Pascal indicated, given the stakes, the limitations of reason, and the possibility of finding eternal happiness by venturing, it makes good sense to leap.[3]

---

[1] Ibid., p. 19.

[2] Kierkegaard, Concluding Unscientific Postscript, p. 384.

[3] Garelick, Anti-Christianity of Kierkegaard, p. 68.

Since the idea of eternal happiness is the highest form of subjectivity, belief in the Paradox is used as a means to reach that degree of subjectivity. Thus, there appears in the <u>Postscript</u> an anti-religious purpose for belief in the Paradox. Subjectivity, for Climacus, is the absolute value, not Christianity:

> Climacus, affirming the paradox because he wants eternal happiness, postulates the right deed but for the wrong reason; this is his religious offense. The justification for acceptance of the Paradox, then, is not the eternal validity of the Paradox itself....Furthermore, using the Paradox as a means to an end violates Climacus' insistence upon the infinite distance between man and God.[1]

Garelick's argument is based upon the limitations of the use of reason in the <u>Postscript</u>. It is only speculative reasoning that Climacus is referring to when he denigrates "reason". In actuality, since reason, i.e., logic, is impotent when confronted with the existential question of the God-man in history, it is reasonable, according to the implicit conclusions derived by Garelick from Climacus' arguments, to believe:

> But to leap at anything when reason admits its limitations, is to give us some real chance at finding eternal happiness; refusing to do so nullifies any chance to succeed.[2]

Garelick's argument relates to my thesis that Kierkegaard is presenting faith as a reasonable enterprise. Garelick is right when he attributes to Climacus the thought that Christianity is a good gamble, a genuine chance at finding eternal happiness. Climacus' reasons for making the movement of faith are

---

[1] <u>Ibid</u>., p. 64.

[2] <u>Ibid</u>., pp. 69-70.

based upon the limitations of speculative reason when confronted with questions of existence--in this case the existence of the God-man in history which, according to Climacus, violates the law of contradiction. As Garelick says:

> To value reason and language as the judge of experience is to end with and only with reason. By its endless process of symbol manufacture, reason creates an opposition between the immediate and symbols, which it then solves by denying the immediate. By fragmenting the immediate, speech and reason gain important practical advantages; however, in doing so we lose experience.
> The arguments Climacus used against language are part of his critique of reason. Reason fails in meeting existential problems....[1]

Although Garelick has not spelled out the distinction between the aesthetic and non-aesthetic works, he has partially captured Kierkegaard's _intended_ meaning in the _Postscript_. It is true that Kierkegaard, through Climacus, is telling us that it makes good sense to leap. Kierkegaard, like Climacus, sees faith as a good gamble, but not strictly in a Pascalian sense. In Kierkegaard's mind, there has been too much speculation regarding faith (Chapter I). In this regard Climacus has served Kierkegaard's purpose. The over-emphasis on doctrinal Christianity must be countered by an attack on reason itself. But the good gamble that Kierkegaard sees in faith is primarily a result of an individual's discovery of despair, as well as of a realization that argumentation regarding the doctrines of faith cannot alone effect an authentic movement of faith. Climacus does not concern himself with this most important preliminary to faith. Kierkegaard's harangues against speculative reason are for the sake of pointing out to aesthetic existents the fact that the beginning of authentic faith orignates with a passionate assessment of self. And we must not forget that irrationality is a mark of the pseudonymous authorship and not Kierkegaard's own position. It is Climacus' view that faith is irrational, not Kierkegaard's. Kierkegaard did not believe that the God-man in history was a logical impossibility. He did not

---

[1] _Ibid._, p. 13.

think that something could be truly illogical, yet existentially possible. As we saw in Chapter I, Kierkegaard does not consider the fact of the God-man in history irrational. He does, however, wish to emphasize the fact that more and more understanding of doctrinal Christianity will not by itself lead to authentic faith. The point is that, as in his other aesthetic works, there are only "telegraphic signals" in <u>Concluding Unscientific Postscript</u> relating to Kierkegaard's real notion of faith and reason. Thus, the <u>fact</u> of Climacus' emphasis upon subjectivity is correctly assessed by Garelick; it is the most important factor in the <u>Postscript</u>. But Climacus' version of subjectivity as being merely a "passionate concern for one's being"[1] is not Kierkegaard's. Genuine subjectivity, for Kierkegaard, is an awareness of the need for a spiritual cure for despair. And subjectivity is not an end in itself, for Kierkegaard, as it is for Climacus in the <u>Postscript</u>. It is the <u>beginning</u> of a spiritual advance from aesthetic living. The emphasis upon passion and inwardness by Kierkegaard is to admonish those who think that abstract reasoning alone can lead to Christian faith.

In regard to the so-called anti-Christian element in the <u>Postscript</u>, Garelick says:

> Whether the <u>Postscript</u> is anti-Christian in a way that was intended by Kierkegaard, and thus Climacus made to serve as a warning to the reader, or whether the anti-Christian conclusion can be attributed to Kierkegaard as well as Climacus, I find a fascinating problem.[2]

I would affirm that an anti-Christian position in regard to the movement of faith can be attributed to Kierkegaard, but not in the way Garelick sees it in Climacus. Climacus was "anti-Christian" in that he used the Paradox to accentuate his own subjectivity as a means to an end. Kierkegaard also sees an anti-religious movement in the movement of faith. Since subjectivity, for Kierkegaard, is to recognize one's deepest spiritual need, i.e., the need for a cure from despair and dread, aesthetic individuals can approach faith no other way than as

---

[1] Ibid., p. 19.

[2] Ibid., pp. 8-9.

viewing it as a means to remedy that need. Faith is a reasonable move for aesthetic existents in that, once their inauthentic state is recognized, the option of faith is seen as a beneficial means to reach the authentic state lacking in their lives. So, for Kierkegaard, reason operates as it does for Climacus, as a resolve to move in the direction of faith once one becomes cognizant of reason's limitation, i.e., logic and speculative thought regarding the doctrines of faith; but it also operates (for Kierkegaard, not Climacus) as the discovery by aesthetic existents of the exclusive alternatives open to those who honestly see their spiritual plight. In this sense, it operates as the ability to judge its own limits in two ways--its ability to judge the reasonableness of acting when there is no strictly logical (the adequate understanding of the tenets of faith which would bring one certainty regarding them) and, more importantly, existential (man's unaided willed efforts) avenues of escape from that state of inauthenticity. Like his other aesthetic works, <u>Concluding Unscientific Postscript</u> does intimate Kierkegaard's own position, but does not easily elucidate it. Garelick sees this, but for the wrong reason. He says:

> Climacus' movement, however, is imperfect. Making Christianity a means, not an end, he violates the absoluteness of religion. In attempting to show the Paradox as the absurd and irrational, he succeeds only in making Christianity a good gamble. The <u>Postscript</u> is a stage to be overcome in the movement to Christianity.[1]

Climacus' movement is imperfect not because the Paradox is treated as a means to an end; rather it is imperfect because Kierkegaard's true notion of subjectivity is not disclosed and all Climacus' assertions of faith as related to it are bound to be imperfect. (Kierkegaard sees aesthetic existents as able to make the movement of faith only as selfish, i.e., viewing it as a means to an end--hence, as beneficial, and reasonable.) Kierkegaard recognizes, even in those who live the life of faith, that accepting the Paradox for its own sake is impossible. (As we saw in Chapter III, Kierkegaard's exposition on the life of faith is one which precludes the possibility of such an acceptance, but not the possibility and even the requirement of Christians approaching that unattainable goal; hence, his emphasis upon the necessity of repeating the act of faith when inevitable, spiritual shortcomings become apparent.) His intent is to have aesthetic existents view faith as that which is beneficial <u>for their own sake</u>, once the work of self-awareness had

---

[1] <u>Ibid</u>., p. 71.

really begun.

B. Kierkegaard's Options

Kierkegaard's aesthetic writings deal with the <u>requirement</u> for belief. There must be a situation which can lead man to decide for faith or against it. Much of the difficulty in assessing Kierkegaard in these works stems from the fact that he is not dealing with the life of faith but with its necessary condition--the situation in which man finds himself confronted with an inescapable choice, i.e., either faith in Christ as a remedy for spiritual death or the continuation of aesthetic living. Thus, Kierkegaard had originally posited subjectivity as the truth so that there might be the <u>beginning</u> of honest introspection in an existent's life. Then, in his psychological works, through his development of the notions of dread and despair, we discover that, for Kierkegaard, subjectivity is untruth. Man, in his most candidly introspective moments, finds that he is dominated by self-centered, sinful interests. His life is primarily one of aesthetic influences. No amount of willed action can ultimately save him from his moral destruction. Finally, then, in Kierkegaard's religious writings and journal entries, his justification for the Christian life comes to the fore. Christ as Healer and Pattern can save men from the inevitable loss of authenticity. It is this awareness based upon the experiences of dread and despair which constitutes true subjectivity.

Man must first see that he desperately <u>needs</u> faith. Personal examination of one's self must precede any authentic movement of faith. That is why Kierkegaard says in a Journal entry:

> I am accused of causing young people to acquiesce in subjectivity. Maybe, for a moment. But how would it be possible to eliminate all the phantoms of objectivity that acts as an audience, etc., except by stressing the category of the separate individual. Under the pretext of objectivity the aim has been to sacrifice individualities entirely. That is the crux of the matter.[1]

---

[1] The Diary of Søren Kierkegaard, ed. Peter P. Rhode, pp. 101-102.

But self-discovery can lead to these two options which Kierkegaard sees as missing from spiritless lives: "This is the situation. Now there can be a question of having faith or of despairing."[1] The discovery of these two mutually exclusive choices by aesthetic individuals and Kierkegaard's hope that individuals will see faith as the reasonable alternative are the very substance of Kierkegaard's endeavor. The fact that they are not easily recognized as such is because of Kierkegaard's pseudonymous authorship. In his journal writings there is ample evidence by Kierkegaard himself of this intent. Kierkegaard hopes, once aesthetic individuals do make a true assessment of self and admit the need for recovery, Christianity can then seem a viable solution:

> Actually, the difficulty is not, when feeling absolutely one's wretchedness, to grasp the consolation of Christianity, to grasp, if I dare say it this way, this matchless exaggeration that God let himself be crucified for my sake in order to save me and to show how he loves me.
> No, the difficulty is to become wretched in this way, to want to risk discovering one's wretchedness.
> To be made well with the aid of Christianity is not the difficulty; the difficulty is in becoming sick to some purpose.
> If you are sick in this way, Christianity comes with matchless ease, just as it is incomparably easy for the starving person to be interested in food....So also with the essentially Christian. If the world disturbs you, then you are not absolutely sick. Imagine that there actually was a hungry person whom everyone would laugh to scorn if he ate the food before him. A few hours very likely would pass by during which he would prefer to be hungry rather than to be laughed to scorn. But if it eventually became a question of death, then he certainly would choose to eat.[2]

---

[1] Søren Kierkegaard's Journals and Papers, Vol. II, p. 20.

[2] Ibid., p. 18.

Then Kierkegaard hopes that individuals can truly view Christianity as reasonable, but not as it would be to the speculative mind:

> There is only one, and quite rightly pathological proof of the truth of Christianity--when the anxiety of sin and the burdened conscience constrain a man to cross the narrow line between despair unto madness--and Christianity.[1]

Kierkegaard sees himself as presenting Christianity in a reasonable light when self-examination is joined to the Christian learning already present:

> Actually, the important thing in reasoning is the ability to see the part within the whole. Most people never actually enjoy a tragedy; it falls into separate pieces for them--nothing but monologues--and an opera into arias etc. The same sort of thing happens in the physical world when, for example, I walk along a road parallel to two other roads with interspersed strips of ground; most people would only see the road, the strip of ground, and then the road but would be unable to see the whole as being like a piece of striped cloth.[2]

The "whole" here is the ability by those of profound spiritual insight to see the value in the Christian movement of faith. And Kierkegaard does see this type of reasoning which results from discovery of self to be of a different <u>kind</u> of reasoning than that which man uses in speculative thought. The important difference is that man has turned within; the options with which reason is confronted result from such introspection. A new kind of knowledge ensues. As he says in regard to Kant and the theories of the pure and practical reason:

---

[1] <u>Ibid.</u>, Vol. I, p. 201.

[2] <u>Ibid.</u>, Vol. II, p. 519.

>....It is therefore probably a mistake for
> the supernaturalist to link his faith to
> the non-knowledge of Kant, because as stated,
> from the nonknowledge of Kant must come
> nonfaith, and the supernaturalist's faith is
> precisely a new consciousness. The error
> appears more clearly in rationalism, which
> remains within the very same limits of
> consciousness, yet without discovering that
> if nonknowledge is admitted in the Kantian
> sense, he can never get faith in his sense
> within the same consciousness, and that the
> only means of attaining faith in this way
> is a more profound investigation of the
> nature of consciousness.[1]

Kierkegaard is saying that if one begins with the fact that the <u>an sich</u> is unknowable, then "nonfaith" results. Only by an initial admission of a more "profound" consciousness, i.e., subjectivity, can faith result.

What Kierkegaard desires is for the aesthetic individual to have the alternatives clearly present so that he can will for that which might effect salvation. Admittedly, this is different from the type of proof in mathematical reasoning:

> A conviction (<u>Overbeviisning</u>) is called a
> conviction because it is <u>over</u> and <u>above</u>
> proof (<u>Beviisning</u>). Proof is given for a
> mathematical proposition in such a way
> that no disproof is conceivable. For that
> reason there can be no conviction with
> respect to mathematics. But as far as
> every existential (<u>existentiel</u>) proposition
> is concerned, for every proof there is
> some disproof, there are a <u>pro</u> and <u>contra</u>.
> The man of conviction is not ignorant of
> this; he knows well enough what doubt is
> able to say: a <u>contra</u>; but nevertheless,
> or more correctly, for that very reason
> he is a man of conviction, because he has
> made a resolution and voluntarily arises

---

[1] <u>Ibid.</u>, Vol. II, p. 523.

himself higher than the dialects of proofs
and is convinced (overbeviist).[1]

But this does not mean that because the will is the final arbiter that reasoning does not have its part to play. It does, and this is why Kierkegaard says:

> If the rights of knowledge are to be given
> their due, we must venture out into life,
> out upon the ocean, and scream in hopes
> that God will hear--we must not stand on the
> shore and watch the others struggle and
> battle--only then does knowledge acquire
> its true <u>official</u> registration.[2]

The life of faith, for Kierkegaard, is the resolution to endure and overcome the onslaughts of despair and dread. Thus, the option of faith is not merely one in which faith in God is presented as a gamble since reason cannot decide <u>pro</u> or <u>contra</u> regarding the doctrines of faith. And there are these added factors which make that option viable: (1) Kierkegaard is addressing nominal Christians who already have a doctrinal belief in Christ and in sin (so his notions of despair and dread are not that foreign, although admittedly more sophisticated in his psychological works than in doctrinal form); and, (2) Kierkegaard sees faith as not just a well-calculated risk, but one which brings, as time goes on, its own reward. Lutherans know well enough that the grace of faith is supposed to convey its own certainty: "....first the venture, then the proof comes afterwards--you will experience that the teaching is true."[3]

Yet, Kierkegaard is cognizant that the option of faith is still a risk. Even with the evidence of the grace of faith, Kierkegaard recognizes this. Yet he believes, on pragmatic grounds alone, that the risk is worth taking:

---

[1] <u>Ibid.</u>, p. 536.

[2] <u>Ibid.</u>, pp. 530-531.

[3] <u>Ibid.</u>, p. 336.

> If someone were to say to the believer: But
> suppose it ends with God's having duped you--
> he would answer with Luther: Be quiet, man,
> God does not do that. And if the person were
> dissatisfied with this answer, he would say:
> Well, all right, if that's the way you want it;
> but I still would not lose anything by con-
> centrating everything on the one thing which
> occupies me. For even if I renounced much in
> this life because I believed it to be God's
> will and it still, as you say, ended with God's
> deceiving me, I still would not have occupied
> myself with getting these things, since either
> I would be aware that God could deceive a man,
> thus that God is a deceiver--that is, that
> everything is nothing--or I would have desisted
> because of concentrating everything on becoming
> involved with God.[1]

Kierkegaard is in no way attempting an argument that would persuade atheists, agnostics, or adherents of another faith. We misunderstand him if this is not clear. The remedy at hand for nominal Christians is a faith that they understand and appreciate, but one to which they are not authentically submitting. The question of another remedy does not arise, especially if faith's certitude becomes evident to the new believer:

> The only conceivable objection would be:
> Yes, but it was still possible that you
> could have been saved in some other way.
> But to this he cannot reply. It is just
> like a person in love. If someone were to
> say: Yes, but you could perhaps have fallen
> in love with another girl--then he must
> answer: To this I cannot reply, for I know
> only one thing, that this is my beloved.
> As soon as the person who is in love can
> reply to this objection, he is then eo ipso
> not in love. And as soon as a believer can
> reply to this objection, he is eo ipso not a
> believer.[2]

---

[1] Ibid., p. 123.

[2] Ibid., Vol. I, p. 201.

C. Kierkegaard's Argument for Faith

We are now in a position to present Kierkegaard's argument as follows:

1) Whether nominal Christians should choose the religious option of faith in Christ cannot be decided by rational inquiry alone, i.e., logic and speculative thought.
2) One is justified in making a decision according to one's wishes that cannot be decided by rational inquiry alone if there is no way to escape the decision and that decision is of monumental importance.
3) If nominal Christians really believe they are inauthentic, that despair is present and that they cannot by their own unaided willed efforts escape from such a state, then they are confronted with the religious options of faith in Christ as a possible remedy or the continuation of their aesthetic existence.

Therefore, if nominal Christians view themselves as inauthentic and desire to make an act of faith in Christ because this option appears more beneficial than the alternative, they are justified in doing so.

Premise one was certainly Kierkegaard's belief. More and more understanding of the doctrines of the Lutheran faith and arguments of a speculative nature can never justify a belief in Christ. There are pros and contras in the matter of Christ's divinity. Premise two refers to Kierkegaard's envisaging genuine faith as an inescapable issue and one in which the will is the final arbiter. Premise three is Kierkegaard's belief that authentic faith in Christ is possible only after an honest assessment of self is effected.

Premise two and three seem acceptable. Premise two refers just to those paramount decisions that are of an either-or nature which cannot be decided by rational, i.e., logical, inquiry alone. It seems reasonable to decide according to what we think best in such cases. Premise three seems incontestable, not because Kierkegaard's psychological thesis is true but if nominal Christians, through self-examination, come to see themselves in the way Kierkegaard has described aesthetic existents. Nor can we contest the fact that if nominal Christians became convinced that they are in the state described, then they would really be confronted with the fact of the potential remedy of Christianity. The persuasiveness of Kierkegaard's argument, then, rests upon premise one. One could argue that the fact of a God-man in history is more improbable then probable, i.e., that the divinity of Christ is part of a mythologizing process etc. Conversely, one could argue, via apologetics, for the _fact_ of the incarnation. Kierkegaard thought otherwise. Christ's divinity is not something that is of the class of being probable or improbable. And, this is not to say that Kierkegaard does not recognize the aesthetic appeal of Christ's life. But, ultimately, the matter of believing must issue from a spiritual need with the knowledge that one is taking a calculated risk which _might_ result in corroboration of another sort, i.e., the grace of faith.

Kierkegaard's appeal to reason is admittedly only implied in his aesthetic works--hence the difficulty in assessing correctly his use of it. When one openly emphasizes the paradox and absurdity of faith, as Kierkegaard did in these pseudonymous works, there is a tendency to judge his other works by them and to forego a careful reading of them. But, as we have seen, there are flagrant inconsistencies in the aesthetic works which could lead us to conclude either that Kierkegaard is an incredibly careless and poor thinker or that he had a method in his madness. Kierkegaard's non-aesthetic works attest to the truth of the latter. He forewarns us not to build a case regarding him _only_ upon the aesthetic works. We have seen that we who are to judge him more than a century after his death benefit from the personal thoughts in his journals concerning this. Yet, such misrepresentation persists. Passing references are made about him as if he is, without question, an irrationalist. Thus, Albert Camus briefly renders this assessment of him based on the denigration of reason in his aesthetic works:

> For him, too, antinomy and paradox become criteria of the religious....Christianity is the scandal, and what Kierkegaard calls for quite plainly is the third sacrifice required by Ignatius Loyola, the one in which God most rejoices: "The sacrifice of the intellect." This effect of the "leap" is odd, but must not surprise us any longer. He makes of the absurd the criterion of the other world, whereas it is simply a residue of the experience of this world.[1]

---

[1] Albert Camus, The Myth of Sisyphus, trans. Justine O'Brien, (New York: Vintage Books, 1955), p. 28.

The charge against Kierkegaard that he views faith as unreasonable is also made by Roderick Chisholm, who bases it only on Climacus' notion of the absurdity of faith in the Postscript:

> The virtue of having faith is thought by some Christians to lie in the very fact that the tenets of the faith are propositions which are not known to be true and which, indeed, are extremely unreasonable.[1]

But, as we have seen, Kierkegaard does not consider the tenets of faith unreasonable. He does, however, think that an analysis of doctrinal Christianity alone cannot yield an authentic movement of faith; the reason for having Climacus relate faith to absurdity is to persuade nominal Christians that it is not understanding the doctrines of faith which is essential Christianity.

Again, we meet criticism of Kierkegaard based on his notion of subjectivity. As we have seen, Kierkegaard does not consider truth synonymous with subjectivity and passion. But one must first be concerned about his spiritual state before one can really understand the true notion of faith. This is Kierkegaard's purpose in emphasizing the notions of passion and subjectivity in the aesthetic works. This purpose is, as we have seen, germane to his real argument for faith. Yet, the case against him is made without putting his notion of subjectivity into proper perspective: Alasdair MacIntyre argues:

> If I hold that truth is subjectivity, what status am I to give to the denial of the proposition that truth is subjectivity? If I produce arguments to refute this denial I appear committed to the view that there are criteria by appeal to which the truth about truth can be vindicated. If I refuse to produce arguments, on the grounds that there can be neither argument nor criteria in such a case, then I appear committed to the view that any view embraced with sufficient subjective passion is as warranted as any other in respect of truth, including the view that truth is not subjectivity. This inescapable dilemma is never faced by Kierkegaard and consequently he remains

---

[1] Roderick M. Chisholm, Theory of Knowledge, (New Jersey: Prentice-Hall, Inc., 1966), p. 14.

trapped by it.[1]

Finally, although it is not the purpose of this work to analyze Kierkegaard's life[2] or to adequately defend him against the charge that his personal life influenced his writings to the degree that we should dismiss all he wrote as the work of a disordered mind, a short comment is in order. Those who use such evidence against him[3] first criticize him on the basis of the aesthetic works without a proper analysis of the non-aesthetic works and the recognition of the place the pseudonymous authorship has in his works; then, because of his notion of the absurdity of faith in the aesthetic works, they claim further that such a notion is the result of an unhappy childhood. But, have such critics been fair? As L. Harold DeWolf has said in Kierkegaard's behalf:

> Whatever a psychiatrist might say about the state of mind from which issued all the great quantity of Kierkegaard's writings, the thoughts he expressed have had a vast and yet increasing influence in philosophy and theology. Many men whose sanity is exemplary find in his writings the highest wisdom. Moreover, even in a wildly disordered dream a man may see the true solution of a problem. The psychological motivation of an utterance is neither proof nor disproof of the ideas expressed.[4]

---

[1] Alasdair MacIntyre, "Existentialism", A Critical History of Western Philosophy, ed. D. J. O'Connor, (New York: The Free Press, 1964), p. 512.

[2] See Walter Lowrie's A Short Life of Kierkegaard, Princeton: Princeton University Press, 1942, for an excellent biography of Kierkegaard.

[3] E. G., Blanshard's "Kierkegaard on Faith", pp. 120-122, and Camus' The Myth of Sisyphus, pp. 28-29, are both examples of arguments which propose that Kierkegaard's advocacy of irrationalism is a product of an unbalanced personality.

[4] L. Harold DeWolf, The Religious Revolt Against Reason, (New York: Harper and Brothers Publishers, 1949), p. 52.

An examination of his religious and journal writings <u>first</u>, before an assessment of the aesthetic works is begun, would be more in order. This, it seems, is seldom done, except by those scholars[1] who have devoted time to the corpus of his works, rather than just to these aesthetic works. As we have noted in this work, criticisms of Kierkegaard are most likely based upon one or two of his aesthetic works, without regard for his journal writings, the religious works and his two psychological treatises. To disregard a great segment of any philosopher's work, especially when we are to judge him regarding that (e.g., the relationship between faith and reason) which pervades all of his works, is poor scholarship. In Kierkegaard's case, are we not justified (<u>a fortiori</u>) in making the same claim?

---

[1] For excellent analyses of Kierkegaard's works, see George E. and George B. Arbaugh, <u>Kierkegaard's Authorship</u>. Illinois: Augustana College Library, 1967; Herman Diem, <u>Kierkegaard</u>. Translated by David Green. Richmond: John Knox Press, 1966; Aage Heinrichson, <u>Kierkegaard Studies in Scandinavia</u>. Copenhagen: Ejnar Munksgaard, 1951; Walter Lowrie, <u>Kierkegaard</u>, 2 Vols. New York: Harper and Brothers, 1962; Gregor Malantschuk, <u>Kierkegaard's Thought</u>. Edited and Translated by Howard V. and Edna H. Hong. Princeton: Princeton University Press, 1971; and Reidar Thomte, <u>Kierkegaard's Philosophy of Religion</u>. Princeton: Princeton University Press, 1949.

BIBLIOGRAPHY

Kierkegaard's Works

Dru, Alexander (ed.). Journals of Kierkegaard. Translated by Alexander Dru. New York: Harper and Row, 1958.

Holmer, Paul (ed.). Edifying Discourses: A Selection. New York: Harper and Row, 1958.

Hong, Howard V. and Edna H. (eds.). Søren Kierkegaard's Journals. Vol. I, A-E and Vol. II, F-K. Bloomington: Indiana University Press, 1967.

Kierkegaard, Søren. Armed Neutrality and An Open Letter. Edited and Translated by Howard V. and Edna H. Hong. New York: Simon and Schuster, 1968.

_____. Attack Upon "Christendom". Translated by Walter Lowrie. Princeton: Princeton University Press, 1968.

_____. Christian Discourses. Translated by Walter Lowrie, Princeton: Princeton University Press, 1971.

_____. The Concept of Dread. Translated by Walter Lowrie. Princeton: Princeton University Press, 1969.

_____. The Concept of Irony. Translated by Lee M. Capel. New York: Harper and Row, 1965.

_____. Concluding Unscientific Postscript. Translated by Walter Lowrie and David F. Swenson. Princeton: Princeton University Press, 1941.

_____. Edifying Discourses. Vol. I and II. Translated by David F. Swenson. Minneapolis: Augsburg Publishing House, 1962.

_____. Either-Or. Vol. I, Translated by David F. and Lillian M. Swenson. Princeton: Princeton University Press, 1941.

_____. Either-Or. Vol. II. Translated by Walter Lowrie. Minneapolis: Augsburg Publishing House, 1962.

_____. Fear and Trembling and The Sickness Unto Death. Translated by David F. Swenson and Lillian M. Swenson. New York: Doubleday and Co., 1941.

_____. For Self-Examination and Judge for Yourselves. Translated by Walter Lowrie. Princeton: Princeton University Press, 1968.

_____. Johannes Climacus or De Omnibus Dubitandum Est. Translated by T. H. Croxall. London: Adam and Charles Black, 1958.

_____. On Authority and Revelation. Translated by Walter Lowrie. New York: Harper and Row, 1966.

_____. Philosophical Fragments. Translated by David F. Swenson, Niels Thulstrup and Howard V. Hong. Princeton: Princeton University Press, 1962.

_____. The Point of View for My Work As An Author: A Report to History. Translated by Walter Lowrie. New York: Harper and Row, 1962.

_____. Purity of Heart. Translated by Douglas V. Steere. New York: Harper and Row, 1956.

_____. Repetition. Translated by Walter Lowrie. New York: Harper and Row, 1964.

_____. Stages on Life's Ways. Translated by Walter Lowrie. New York: Schocken Books, 1967.

_____. Training in Christianity. Translated by Walter Lowrie. Princeton: Princeton University Press, 1967.

_____. Works of Love. Translated by David F. and Lillian M. Swenson. Princeton: Princeton University Press, 1946.

Rhode, Peter (ed). The Diary of Søren Kierkegaard.
    Translated by Gerde M. Hendersen. New York: The
    Polyglot Press, 1960.

Secondary Sources

Books

Arbaugh, George E. and George B. Kierkegaard's Authorship.
    Illinois: Augustana College Library, 1967.

Auden, W. H. The Living Thought of Kierkegaard.
    Bloomington: Indiana University Press, 1946.

Barrett, William. Irrational Man. New York: Doubleday
    and Co., 1958.

_____. What is Existentialism? New York:
    Grove Press, 1964.

Blackham, N. J. Six Existential Thinkers. New York:
    Harper and Row, 1959.

Camus, Albert. The Myth of Sisyplus. New York: Vintage
    Books, 1955.

Carnell, Edward. The Burden of Søren Kierkegaard.
    Michigan: William D. Eerdmans Publishing Co., 1965.

Chisholm, Roderick M. Theory of Knowledge. New Jersey:
    Prentice-Hall, Inc., 1966.

Collins, James. The Mind of Kierkegaard. Chicago:
    Henry Regnery Co., 1967.

Copleston, Frederick. History of Philosophy. Vol. VII.
    New York: Doubleday and Co., 1965.

DeWolf, Harold. The Religious Revolt Against Reason.
    New York: Harper and Brothers, 1949.

Diem, Hermann. Kierkegaard. Translated by David Green.
    Richmond: John Knox Press, 1966.

_____. Kierkegaard's Dialectic of Existence.
Translated by Harold Knight. New York: Frederick
Ungar Publishing Co., 1965.

Dupre, Louis. Kierkegaard As Theologian. New York:
Sheed and Ward, 1963.

Garelick, Herbert M. The Anti-Christianity of Kierkegaard.
The Hague: Martinus Nijhoff, 1965.

Hamilton, Kenneth. The Promise of Kierkegaard. Philadelphia: J. B. Lippincourt Co., 1969.

Heinrichson, Aage. Kierkegaard Studies in Scandanavia.
Copenhagen: Ejnar Munksgaard, 1951.

Heywood, Thomas. Subjectivity and Paradox. New York:
The MacMillan Co., 1957.

Kaufmann, Walter. Existentialism from Dostoevsky to Sartre.
Cleveland: The World Publishing Co., 1956.

Lawson, Lewis (ed). Kierkegaard's Presence in Contemporary
American Life: Essays for Various Disciplines.
New Jersey: The Scandinavian Press, 1967.

Lowrie, Walter. Kierkegaard, 2 Vols. New York: Harper
and Brothers, 1962.

_____. A Short Life of Kierkegaard. Princeton:
Princeton University Press, 1942.

Mackey, Louis. A Kind of Poet. Philadelphia: University
of Pennsylvania Press, 1971.

Malantschuk, Gregor. Kierkegaard's Thought. Edited and
Translated by Howard V. and Edna H. Hong. Princeton:
Princeton University Press, 1971.

Perkins, Robert. Søren Kierkegaard. Richmond: John Knox
Press, 1969.

Price, George. The Narrow Pass: A Study of Kierkegaard's
Concept of Man. New York: McGraw Hill Book Co.,
1963.

Prosch, Harry. *The Genesis of Twentieth Century Philosophy.* New York: Doubleday and Co., 1966.

Schraeder, George. *Existential Philosophers: Kierkegaard to Merleau-Ponty.* New York: McGraw Hill Co., 1967.

Sponheim, Paul. *Kierkegaard on Christ and Christian Coherence.* New York: Harper and Row, 1968.

Sweeney, Leo. *A Metaphysics of Authentic Existentialism.* Princeton: Princeton University Press, 1965.

Swenson, David. *Something About Kierkegaard.* Minneapolis: Augsburg Publishing House, 1945.

Thomte, Reidar. *Kierkegaard's Philosophy of Religion.* Princeton: Princeton University Press, 1949.

Wild, John. *The Challenge of Existentialism.* Bloomington: Indiana University Press, 1966.

Williams, J. Rodman. *Contemporary Existentialism and Christian Faith.* New Jersey: Prentice-Hill Inc., 1965.

Wolf, Herbert. *Kierkegaard and Bultmann: The Quest of the Historical Jesus.* Minneapolis: Augsburg Publishing House, 1965.

Periodicals and Essays

Allison, H. E. "Christianity and Nonsense", *Review of Metaphysics*, XX, No. 3 (March, 1967), 432-460.

Blanshard, Brand. "Kierkegaard on Faith", *Essays on Kierkegaard.* Edited by Jerry H. Gill. Minneapolis: Burgess Publishing Co., 1965, 113-126.

Campbell, Richard. "Lessing's Problem and Kierkegaard's Answer", *Essays on Kierkegaard.* Edited by Jerry H. Gill. Minneapolis: Burgess Publishing Co., 1965, 74-89.

Clive, G. "Sickness Unto Death in the Vacenworld: A Study of Nihilism", *Harvard Theological Review*, LI (July, 1958), 135-167.

Collins, James. "Faith and Reflection in Kierkegaard", A Kierkegaard Critique. Edited by Howard A. Johnson and Niels Thulstrup. New York: Harper and Brothers, 1962, 22-39.

Diem, Hermann. "Kierkegaard's Bequest to Theology", A Kierkegaard Critique. Edited by Howard A. Johnson and Niels Thulstrup. New York: Harper and Brothers, 1962, 244-255.

Dietrichson, Paul. "Introduction to a Reappraisal of Fear and Trembling", Inquiry, XII (Summer, 1969), 236-245.

Eller, V. "Fact, Faith and Foolishness: Kierkegaard and the New Quest", Journal of Religion, XLVIII (January 1968), 54-68.

Fabro, Cornelio. "Faith and Reason in Kierkegaard's Dialectics", A Kierkegaard Critique. Edited by Howard A. Johnson and Niels Thulstrup. New York: Harper and Brothers, 1962, 156-206.

Fitzpatrick, M. "Current Kierkegaard Study-Whence?-Whither?", Journal of Religion, L (January, 1970), 79-90.

Gerber, R. J. "Kierkegaard's Reason and Faith", Thought, XLIV (Spring, 1969), 29-52.

Gill, Jerry. "Kant, Kierkegaard and Religious Knowledge", Essays on Kierkegaard. Minneapolis: Burgess Publishing Co., 1965, 6-30.

Hamilton, Kenneth. "Man: Anxious or Guilty? A Second Look at Kierkegaard's Concept of Dread", Essays on Kierkegaard. Edited by Jerry Gill. Minneapolis: Burgess Publishing Co., 1965, 167-174.

Hartt, J. N. "Christian Freedom Reconsidered: The Case of Kierkegaard", Harvard Theological Review, LX (April, 1967), 133-144.

Held, M. "Historical Kierkegaard: Fact or Gnosis", Journal of Religion, XXXVIII (October, 1957), 260-266.

Herbert, R. "Two of Kierkegaard's Uses of Paradox", Philosophical Review, LXX (January, 1961), 41-55.

Holmer, Paul. "On Understanding Kierkegaard", A Kierkegaard Critique. Edited by Howard A. Johnson and Niels Thulstrup. New York: Harper and Brothers, 1962, 40-53.

_____. "Theology and Belief", Essays on Kierkegaard. Edited by Jerry H. Gill. Minneapolis: Burgess Publishing Co., 1965, 186-197.

Jansen, F. J. B. "Universality of Kierkegaard", American Scandinavian Review, LI (June, 1963), 145-149.

Klemke, E. D. "Logicality vs. Alogicality in The Christian Faith", Journal of Religion, XXXVIII, No. 1 (April, 1958), 107-115.

_____. "Some Misinterpretations of Kierkegaard", Hibbert, LXVIII (April, 1959), 250-270.

Larsen, R. E. "Kierkegaard's Absolute Paradox", Journal of Religion, XLII (January, 1962), 24-43.

Lindstrom, Valter. "The Problem of Objectivity and Subjectivity in Kierkegaard", A Kierkegaard Critique. Edited by Howard A. Johnson and Niels Thulstrup. New York: Harper and Brothers, 1962, 228-243.

MacIntyre, Alasdair. "Existentialism", A Critical History of Western Philosophy. Edited by D. J. O'Connor. New York: The Free Press, 1964.

_____. "Kierkegaard, Søren Aabye", The Encyclopedia of Philosophy. Vol. IV. Editor in Chief Paul Edwards. New York: The Free Press, 1967, 336-340.

Mackey, Louis. "Kierkegaard and the Problem of Existential Philosophy", Essays on Kierkegaard. Edited by Jerry H. Gill. Minneapolis: Burgess Publishing Co., 1965, 31-57.

_____. "Loss of the World in Kierkegaard's Ethics", Journal of Philosophy. LVIII (October, 1961), 701.

McKinnon, Alistair. "Believing the Paradoks: A Contradiction in Kierkegaard?", Harvard Theological Review, LXI (October, 1968), 633-636.

_____. "Kierkegaard's Irrationalism Revisited", International Philosophical Quarterly, IX, No. 2 (June, 1969), 165-176.

_____. "Kierkegaard's Pseudonyms: A New Hierarchy", American Philosophical Quarterly, VI, No. 2 (April, 1969), 116-124.

Michalson, C. "Theology of Faith", Religion in Life, XXXII (Spring, 1963), 225-237.

Murphy, Arthur E. "On Kierkegaard's Claim That 'Truth is Subjectivity'", Essays on Kierkegaard. Edited by Jerry H. Gill. Minneapolis: Burgess Publishing Co., 1965, 94-101.

Paul, W. W. "Fact and Reason in Kierkegaard and Modern Existentialism", Review of Metaphysics, XX (March, 1956), 149-163.

Rhode, Peter. "Søren Kierkegaard: The Father of Existentialism", Essays on Kierkegaard. Edited by Jerry H. Gill. Minneapolis: Burgess Publishing Co., 1965, 6-30.

Schmitt, R. "Kierkegaard's Ethics and Its Teleological Suspension", Journal of Philosophy, LVIII (October, 1961), 701.

Schrag, C. O. "Note on Kierkegaard's Teleological Suspension of the Ethical", Ethics, LXX (October, 1959), 66-68.

Søe, N. H. "Kierkegaard's Doctrine of the Paradox", A Kierkegaard Critique. Edited by Howard A. Johnson and Niels Thulstrup. New York: Harper and Brothers, 1962, 207-227.

Sontag, Frederick. "Kierkegaard and the Search for a Self", Essays on Kierkegaard. Edited by Herry H. Gill. Minneapolis: Burgess Publishing Co., 1965, 175-185.

Thulstrup, Niels. "The Complex of Problems Called Kierkegaard", A Kierkegaard Critique. Edited by Howard A. Johnson and Niels Thulstrup. New York: Harper and Brothers, 1962, 286-296.

Walker, Jeremy. "Kierkegaard's Concept of Truthfulness", Inquiry. XII (Summer, 1969), 209-234.

Wild, John. "Kierkegaard and Contemporary Existentialist Philosophy", A Kierkegaard Critique. Edited by Howard A. Johnson and Niels Thulstrup. New York: Harper and Brothers, 1962, 22-39.